SECRETS OF DANIEL

To order additional copies of
Secrets of Daniel, by Jacques B. Doukhan, call 1-800-765-6955

Visit our website at *www.rhpa.org* for information on other
Review and Herald products.

SECRETS OF DANIEL

Wisdom and Dreams of a Jewish Prince in Exile

Jacques B. Doukhan

REVIEW AND HERALD® PUBLISHING ASSOCIATION
HAGERSTOWN, MD 21740

The author assumes full responsibility for the accuracy of all facts and
quotations as cited in this book.

This book was
Edited by Gerald Wheeler
Copyedited by Delma Miller and James Cavil
Designed by Willie Duke
Electronic makeup by Shirley M. Bolivar
Typeset: Bembo 12/14

PRINTED IN U.S.A.

04 03 02 01 00   5 4 3 2 1

R&H Cataloging Service
Doukhan, Jacques B
    Secrets of Daniel: Wisdom and dreams of a Jewish prince
in exile

    1. Bible. O.T. Daniel—Commentaries.   1. Title.

                    224.5

ISBN: 0-8280-1424-8

CONTENTS

PROLOGUE

The small Iraqi village was in turmoil as people hurled insults and maledictions from one side to the other of the Touster River.[1] Women wailed and cursed. Men sharpened their knives. Children trembled. At the dawn of another Middle Eastern conflict, the problem was not a question of oil or of Jews versus Arabs, but an old legend concerning Daniel's coffin.

Ancient belief regarded the bones of the prophet as an omen of good luck. Observing that the inhabitants on the bank where lay the prophet's tomb were prosperous and happy, while those on the other side were unhappy and poor, the latter naturally sought to have the tomb transferred to their side of the river. The conflict was about to explode when, after much discussion, a compromise settled the matter: the villagers would move the coffin every other year to the other bank, so as to benefit both sides. The practice lasted several years until the visit of King Sagarschah, who thought the frequent disinterments dishonored the memory of the prophet. Under his supervision the villagers chained the coffin to the middle of a bridge at an equal distance from both banks. Daniel was then for everybody.

This story, as told by a twelfth-century traveler,[2] echoes on. A small 12-chapter document lost in the folds of the ancient Bible and the only actual remains of the ancient prophet, the book of Daniel contains a universal message that transcends denominations and cultures. The book of Daniel concerns all of us.

Already Judaism recognized Daniel, according to the testimony of Flavius Josephus, as "one of the greatest prophets," as "he was not only wont to prophesy future things, as did the other prophets, but he also fixed the time at which these would come to pass."[3]

References to the book of Daniel appear in the intertestamental literature (100-200 B.C.E.)[4] and in the legends of the time,[5] and its influence on the community of Qumran[6] all testify to the same veneration.

The Talmud admires Daniel as one who would outweigh "all the wise men of other nations."[7] The Midrash considers Daniel and Jacob as the only two recipients of an end-of-time revelation from God.[8] According to another Midrash, God disclosed to Daniel the destiny of Israel and the date of the last judgment.[9] In spite of some reservations resulting from Judeo-Christian polemic, the prophecies of Daniel remain the object of intense study on the part of Jewish scholars. The great Maimonides applied them to Rome, Greece, Persia, Islam, and even to Christianity.[10] Renowned scholars such as the exegete Rashi, the head of the community Saadia Gaon, the poet and philosopher Nachmanides, the politician Abrabanel, and the humanist Loeb (Maharal) all have pondered the book of Daniel and attempted to derive from it the date of the coming of the Messiah.[11] More recently, in the twentieth century, the philosopher Franz Rosenzweig did not hesitate to establish a link between the history of the world and the prophecy of Daniel.[12] Abraham Heschel cited Daniel as the prophet in waiting,[13] and André Neher qualified him as the "prophet of prayer." For Elie Wiesel, the book of Daniel contains the flower of hope.[14]

The Christian tradition regards Daniel as a prophet of reference. It is often on the basis of the book of Daniel that the early Christians fleshed out their argumentation and testimony. The book attracted the interest of Christian philosophers such as Hippolytus, Jerome, and even Thomas Aquinas.[15] Later the Reformation produced a flood of commentaries and studies on the book of Daniel. According to Luther, working then on his translation of the Scriptures, the book of Daniel deserves to be published first.[16] It later became the central theme of Calvin's most brilliant conferences.[17] During the nineteenth-century religious renewal movement, the book of Daniel inspired Messianic expectations.[18] Today the book of Daniel is again the object of a resurgence of studies.[19]

Even Islam has had an interest in the book of Daniel. The Islamic tradition has retained most of the episodes of the life of *Daniyal*, otherwise known as the "great judge and viceroy" (Daniel at the court of Nebuchadnezzar, in the lions' den, Nebuchadnezzar's folly, the feast of Nebuchadnezzar, etc.). But even here, Islam remembers Daniel especially as a prophet who predicts the future and the end of the world. The Koran refers to the prophecies of Daniel through the dream of *Dhul Quarnain* (the two horns), probably based on the vision of Daniel 8. In the Middle Ages the Muslims conceived popular horoscopes *(malhamat Daniyal)* whose authority they attributed to Daniel. Islam also associates the prophecies of Daniel with the memory of the great Caliph Omar.[20] More recently, the Baha'i movement, emerging from Iranian Shiism, justifies its existence on the basis of the prophecy of Daniel. Baha'i scholars believe that the twelfth *Bab* or *Mahdi,* who is awaited in Iranian Islam as the restorer of an era of peace and justice, has already come in 1844 of our era (1260 of the hegira of Mohammad). They base their conclusion on the 1260-day prophecy of Daniel.[21]

Beyond the religious traditions, philosophers such as Spinoza, psychologists such as Jung, and scientists such as Newton have paid special attention to Daniel,[22] and the book has even inspired the poet and the artist. From the bare paraphrase of Middle Ages liturgical drama to the elaborate compositions of Darius Milhaud, to the hoarse melodies of Louis Armstrong, the themes in Daniel have taken multiple forms: seventeenth-century tragicomedies, the cantata, and twentieth-century jazz.[23] Painters have drawn inspiration from it. Michelangelo, Rembrandt, Rubens, Delacroix,[24] among others, have created masterpieces that not only depict the extraordinary scenes of miracle, but also dare to develop the prophetic cycles. Indeed, the book of Daniel does not exclusively belong to the religious tradition but also to the secular heritage. In fact, we may perceive the universal character of the book of Daniel from within the work itself.

Undeniably, the book of Daniel is first and foremost a religious book. However, its spiritual depth seems to pale next to its fantastic and dazzling apocalyptic visions and miracles. In reality, the structure of the book of Daniel closely links the sensational to the daily rhythm of prayer. The book mentions seven prayers. Some are more implicit through the traditional gesture of prostrating oneself toward

Jerusalem. Others are explicit and enunciated. Profound and of moving beauty, they are always rooted in the historical event, in the human experience. The longest of the prayers appears in the ninth chapter, precisely between two prophecies: one concerning the 70 years of Jeremiah, which announces the return of Israel from exile; the other, of 70 weeks, which speaks of the restoration of Jerusalem and of the world's salvation. This entwining of prayer with historical event is typical of the biblical concept of the spiritual. In the Bible, meeting the divine does not imply detachment from the real. On the contrary, the two experiences are interrelated. History rests in the hands of prayer.

And because it is incarnated, the spirituality of Daniel is human. The book offers itself also in poetry, employing poetic devices such as parallelisms, echoes, plays on words, and rhythms. The reader will need to recognize such literary devices in order to grasp the subtle meaning of the words. For in this book, beauty is truth, though it does not imply that rational and philosophical truth are secondary. In fact, the book of Daniel beckons to our thoughts and intelligence. A book of wisdom, it contains the most profound thoughts on history, God, ethics, and existence. The Hebrew canon inserts the book of Daniel among the books of Wisdom. It presents Daniel himself as a wise man (Dan. 1:20; 2:13). That is, he is a man capable of understanding. The book presents truth as something to be understood. Significantly, the verb "to understand" is one of the key words in the book of Daniel. Daniel tries to "understand" (see Dan. 9:13). The angel makes Daniel "understand" the visions (see Dan. 8:17; 9:22, 23). It may even happen that Daniel remains "without understanding" (see Dan. 8:27). Finally, the book urges the people of God to "understand and to bring others to understanding" (see Dan. 11:32, 33). Mathematical figures riddle the prophecy of Daniel, a rare occurrence in the Bible. The prediction of an event follows the rigor of scientific thought. André Lacocque was right in declaring that "one of the most important contributions of the book of Daniel is its novel insistence on the linking of faith to understanding."[25] Such "emphasis" on intelligence can seem paradoxical in the context of revelation, as faith often seems opposed to intelligence.

The book of Daniel teaches us that intelligence and thought are prerequisite. Yet it also presents itself as a challenge to intelligence, as its words remain "sealed" (Dan. 12:4, 9).

In addition to the traditional language of Hebrew, Daniel employs Aramaic (Dan. 2:4 to 7:28), the international language of that epoch, as well as some words deriving from ancient Babylonian (Akkadian), Persian, and even Greek. This multiplicity of tongues in the book of Daniel is a unique example of a message that pushes through the borders of Israel and offers itself to the intelligence of the nations.

The universal character of the book also appears in the content itself. It is a religious work that speaks in the name of God and reveals the vision from above as well as a historical work that refers to past, present, and future. Beyond that, it is a book of prayers surging forth from a man who trembles before his Creator; a book of poetry that displays the priceless beauty of its songs. Yet it is also a work of wisdom and enigmas that provoke and stimulate thought and intelligence. The religious person, the mystical one, as well as the scientist and philosopher, the Jew like the Gentile—all find themselves drawn to its content. The book of Daniel is universal and deserves the attention of all.

---

[1] A small river east of the Tigris River (formerly the Choaspes).

[2] See A. Asher, *The Itinerary of Benjamin of Tudele* (in Hebrew) (London: 1840-1841), Vol. I, pp. 152-154.

[3] Josephus *Antiquities of the Jews* 10. 266, 267.

[4] See Esdras 12:11, the book of Enoch (83-90), the Sibylline oracles (4:388-400), 1 Maccabees (1:54; 2:59ff.), the Testaments of the Twelve Patriarchs, Jubilees, the Apocalypse of Baruch, etc.

[5] See especially the inserted passages in the Septuagint Bible (the prayer of Azariah, the hymn of the three young men, the story of Susannah, and the episode of Bel and the Dragon). The Catholic Church retained these Greek texts (Deuterocanicals), absent from the Hebrew Bible, but not by the churches of the Reformation, who referred to them as the Apocrypha.

[6] The book of Daniel was undoubtedly a favorite of the Qumran sect. Archaeologists have recovered several manuscripts, some containing almost all the chapters of the book, and an important number of passages (from chapters 1, 5, 7, 8, 10, and 11) appear in duplicate. (See A. Dupont-Sommer, *The Essene Writings From Qumran,* trans. G. Vermes (Gloucester, Mass.: 1973); E. Ulich, "Daniel Manuscripts From Qumran, part 1: Preliminary Editions of 4QDan (b) and 4QDan (c)," *Bulletin of the American Schools of Oriental Research* 268 (1987): 3-16; "Daniel Manuscripts From Qumran, part 2: Preliminary Editions of 4QDan (b) and 4QDan (c)," *Bulletin of the American Schools of Oriental Research* 274 (1989): 3-26.

[7] Babylonian Talmud *Yoma* 77a.

[8] Midrash Choher *Tov* 31. 7.

[9] Midrash Rabbah *Genesis* 98. 2.

[10] *Iggeret Teman* IV, V.

[11] For references to these authors, see Dan Cohn-Sherbok, *The Jewish Messiah* (Edinburgh: 1997), pp. 119, 120.

[12] See Franz Rosenzweig, *The Star of Redemption,* trans. William W. Hallo (New York: 1970), p. 336.

[13] Abraham J. Heschel, *Israel: An Echo of Eternity* (New York: 1969), p. 97.

[14] Concerning the book of Daniel, Elie Wiesel writes: "I love to read and reread it. Because of its beauty? Because of its danger? Indeed, it is impossible to decipher its secret, but at least we know it has a secret—this knowledge helps us to go beyond the common and to reject vulgarity. This knowledge enables us to give hope a name which precedes Creation itself" (*Sages and Dreamers* [New York: 1991], p. 114).

[15] For references to these authors, see James A. Montgomery, *A Critical and Exegetical Commentary on the Book of Daniel* (New York: 1927), pp. 107, 108.

[16] *Vorrede über den Propheten Daniel,* 1530, rev. 1541 (Deutsche Bibel, 1960), p. 13.

[17] John Calvin, *Commentaries on the Book of the Prophet Daniel,* trans. Thomas Myers (Grand Rapids: 1948), vol. 1.

[18] See Henri Desroche, *The Sociology of Hope,* trans. Carol Martin-Sperry (London/Boston/Henley: 1979).

[19] See André Lacocque, *The Book of Daniel,* trans. David Pellauer (Atlanta: 1979); the massive bibliography in John E. Goldingay, *Word Biblical Commentary, Daniel,* vol. 30 (Dallas: 1989), pp. XXI-XXIV, XLI-LIII; and A. S. van der Woude, ed., *The Book of Daniel in the Light of New Findings* (Leuven: 1993).

[20] See G. Vajda, "Dāniyāl," in *The Encyclopedia of Islam,* new ed., ed. B. Lewis, Ch. Pellat and J. Schacht (Leiden: 1965), p. 112.

[21] See Shoghi Effendi, *God Passes By,* with an introduction by George Townshend (Wilmette, Ill.: 1970), pp. 57, 58.

[22] Baruch Spinoza, *Tractatus Theologico-Politicus,* trans. Samuel Shirley (Leiden/New York/København/Köln: 1989), p. 189; C. G. Jung, *Dreams,* trans. R. F. Hull (Princeton: 1974), p. 37; Isaac Newton, *Observations Upon the Prophecies of Daniel and the Apocalypse of St. John* (London: 1733).

[23] A "Daniel Drama" composed in the twelfth century by Hilarius, disciple of Abelard (Paris: Bibl. Nat. 11331, vol. 12-16) and in the thirteenth century by the Beauvais Cathedral School (London, Brit. Mus. Egerton 2615, vol. 95-108); Darius Milhaud, *Les Miracles de la foi,* 1951; the Negro spiritual "Shadrac," composed in 1931 by Mac Gimsey (best-seller record, 1938, by Louis Armstrong and his orchestra); the German play *Der Siegende Hofmann Daniel,* 1671; Vachel Lindsay, *The Daniel Jazz,* put to music by Louis Gruenberg in 1923.

[24] A painting *Daniel* among the frescoes of the Sistine Chapel in the Vatican (1508-1512)—a postage stamp of it appeared in 1961; *Vision of Daniel* (1652), at the national museum of Berlin; *Daniel and the Lions* (1618), National Gallery of Art, Washington, D.C.; *Daniel dans la fosse aux lions* (1849), at the Bourbon Palace in Paris.

[25] Lacocque, p. 191.

CHAPTER 1

INTRODUCTION
THE VICTORY OF BABYLON

The book of Daniel opens with a military clash: Babylon against Jerusalem: "In the third year of the reign of Jehoiakim king of Judah, Nebuchadnezzar king of Babylon came to Jerusalem and besieged it" (Dan. 1:1).

Beyond the local skirmish that involves the two historical kingdoms, the author points to yet another conflict—a universal one. The classical association "Babylon-Jerusalem" already suggests such a reading of the text, and it receives further confirmation through the evocation of Shinar (verse 2), mythical name of Babylon and related to the biblical episode of Babel (Gen. 11:2). Ever since the most ancient times Babylon has symbolized in the Bible the forces of evil that oppose God and seek to possess divine prerogatives and privileges.

The narrative of Genesis 11:1-9 relates how in the days following the Flood, humanity decided to build a tower that would lead them to heaven's gates. The text then tells, not without humor, of God's shattering descent to disrupt their project by confounding their language. In a play on words, Scripture explains the name of Babel in relation to the root *bll,* which means "to confuse" (verse 9). Therefore, Babel, the Hebrew word for Babylon, is the biblical symbol for the world below usurping power that belongs exclusively to the one above.

Later the prophets will again use this theme as the Babylonian threat becomes more precise:

"You will take up this taunt against the king of Babylon: . . . You said in your heart, 'I will ascend to heaven; I will raise my throne above the stars of God; I will sit enthroned on the mount of assembly, on the utmost heights of the sacred mountain. I will ascend above the tops of the clouds; I will make myself like the Most High'" (Isa. 14:4-14; cf. Jer. 50:17-40; Eze. 31).

Behind the confrontation between Babylon and Jerusalem the prophets see a conflict of another dimension. We must read the book of Daniel then with this perspective in mind.

I. The Deportation (Dan. 1:2)

The book primarily denounces the Exile as a movement of usurpation on Babylon's part. The people of God and the sacred articles of the Temple now become Nebuchadnezzar's property: "And the Lord delivered Jehoiakim king of Judah into his hand [Nebuchadnezzar], along with some of the articles from the temple of God" (verse 2). A fuller understanding of these words necessitates a quick overview of their historical context.

We are in 605 B.C.E.[1] The Chaldeans have besieged Jerusalem, the capital of Judah, and deported its inhabitants. A century before (722 B.C.E.) the Assyrians had invaded the northern kingdom of Israel (2 Kings 17:3-23). The kingdom of Judah therefore represents the last surviving portion of the ancient Davidic kingdom.

After the death of Solomon the kingdom of David had split in two. The 10 northern tribes became the northern kingdom of Israel, and the two southern tribes formed the kingdom of Judah. Following the schism, in spite of fratricidal conflicts, the external history of the two kingdoms presented about the same characteristics. Situated between the two superpowers of Egypt in the south and Assyria in the north, Israel as well as Judah often found itself tempted to ally itself with the southern superpower in order to resist the northern one. Both kingdoms will experience the same fate as the ill-fated alliance precipitates their downfall.

In Israel the king Hoshea sought diplomatic, military, and other ties with Egypt in the hope of shaking off the Assyrian yoke. The Assyrian response was immediate. It occupied the territory of Israel and arrested and imprisoned Hoshea (verses 4, 5). Samaria, the capital, resisted for three years, then succumbed in 722 B.C.E. The king of Assyria, Sargon II, employed the practice of deportation already inaugurated by Tiglath-pileser III (745-727 B.C.E.). Sargon forcefully transferred the Israelites to the eastern regions of Assyria and replaced them with Assyrian settlers of Babylonian origin and by Kutheans—the future Samaritans. The majority of the Hebrew people disappear in the process. Ten tribes out of 12 assimilate into the Assyrian population. The kingdom of Judah, with its two tribes, survives for some time but ultimately experiences the same outcome, and the Judean tribes find themselves forced into exile. However, now the Babylonians have replaced the Assyrians. Assyria has long since vanished, its capital, Nineveh, destroyed in 612 B.C.E. Furthermore, the Judeo-Egyptian alliance was not as spontaneous as the Israeli-Egyptian one. In fact, the Egyptians imposed it in the course of a military campaign during which they replaced the Judean king, Jehoahaz, then allied to Babylon, with his brother, Jehoiakim, of a more docile nature (2 Kings 23:31-24:7; 2 Chron. 36:1-4). Babylon, not pleased with the events, considered Judean territory as its own. Three years later, the aging king of Babylon, Nabopolassar, sent his son Nebuchadnezzar against the Egyptian armies. The encounter took place at Carchemish in the year 605 B.C.E. Defeating the Egyptian armies, Nebuchadnezzar scours the land of Israel and subjugates Jehoiakim, but the news of his father's death precipitates his return. He hurries back, taking with him young captives from the elite of Judah, including Daniel and his companions. Nebuchadnezzar, knowing he must quickly secure his throne from usurpers, takes, with some trusted forces, the shortcut across the desert. The prisoners and the rest of the army follow the normal more hospitable trade route to the north. Chained and uprooted, the Judeans have lost everything. Their past, their hope, their identities, their values, all is compromised. In exile it is easy to forget one's homeland. In fact, the strategy behind deportation is to exile the inhabitants in order to subjugate them better. Minorities, lost in the indigenous population, become so concerned with the need to adjust that they do not have opportunity to rebel. And who knows, they might even assimilate and become like the others around them.

The ordeal, however, involves a wider scope than the personal discomfort of an exiled minority: the end of Judah means the disappearance of the last sons of Jacob. It is a fate that concerns the chosen people, hence its spiritual and cosmic connotation. The removal of the last witness of God jeopardizes the survival of the world. Babylon has replaced Jerusalem, and one cannot ignore the religious implications of such a usurpation. Significantly, the text underlines three times Nebuchadnezzar's appropriation of the utensils of God's Temple for his own temple use: "These he carried off to the temple of his god in Babylonia and put in the treasure house of his god" (Dan. 1:2).

Nebuchadnezzar has replaced the God of Judah. Worse yet, the event itself is a judgment by God: "The Lord delivered . . . into his hand" (verse 2). As a result, we witness the fulfillment of the prophecies uttered by the ancient prophets of Israel as both a warning and a call for repentance (Isa. 39:5-7; Jer. 20:5).

II. Cultural Alienation (Dan. 1:3-7)

Upon the Judeans' arrival in Babylon, the king's officials immediately take charge of them. After careful screening by the chief eunuch, the Babylonian administrators carefully select young men of royal blood (verse 3) in perfect physical condition and superior intellect to be trained for the king's service.[2] Those chosen include the prince Daniel, probably a direct descendant of Zedekiah, the last king of Judah.[3] That the chief eunuch[4] Ashpenaz is in charge of the screening operation hints at the painful tragedy of the new captives. It may well be that Daniel and his companions underwent castration and became eunuchs to serve at the royal court, a common practice in the ancient Near East, as evidenced by Assyrian carvings of court life. Thus the upper-class eunuch slaves were often exiled men of foreign origin. As the princes of Judah underwent the humiliating procedure, they may have remembered Isaiah's prophecy (Isa. 39:7) that predicted that the offspring of Hezekiah would become eunuchs at the Babylonian court.

The young men immediately entered the best Chaldean schools.

16

It involved much more than merely a technical initiation to Babylonian literature and script. It required a minimum of three languages to function as a scribe: Sumerian, the traditional sacred tongue written in cuneiform signs; Babylonian (or Akkadian), the national dialect of Semitic origin, also in cuneiform; and finally, Aramaic, the international language of business and diplomacy, written much like the letter forms that we encounter in modern Hebrew Bibles. The magical techniques of the Chaldeans were also an important part of the curriculum. Already the word "Chaldean" renders this function. Derived from the Babylonian root *kaldu* (or *kashdu*), it alludes to "the art of constructing astronomical maps," a specialty of the Chaldeans. The Babylonians were masters in astronomy. Ancient documents relate observations and even predictions of eclipses with remarkable precision (such as one in 747 B.C.E.). But this science had another goal than the mere determination of astronomical movement. Ultimately, what such celestial scanning sought was to be able to predict the future. The Chaldean astronomer was above all an astrologer. Today's horoscope tradition traces back to Babylonian times. It was the Babylonian's belief, not unlike that of many of our contemporaries, that astral movement determined human destiny. The curriculum of the scribal apprentices thus essentially had a religious nature and was designed to turn the Hebrews into genuine Chaldean priests, experts in the science of divination.

The goal of cultural transformation did not limit itself to the intellectual domain but touched the most intimate aspects of everyday life, including the diet. Thus the king "determines" the menu. The verb used here in the form *wayeman* (determined) has in the Bible no other subject but God Himself and appears otherwise only in a creation context (Jonah 1:17; 4:6-8). The unexpected use of that verb in relation to Nebuchadnezzar suggests that the king in "determining" the menu takes the place of the Creator. A more careful observation of the meals reveals the king's intentions. Indeed, the "meat-wine" association characterizes both in the Bible and in ancient Middle Eastern cultures the ritual meal taken in the context of a worship service. To participate in such a meal implied submission to the Babylonian cult and recognition of Nebuchadnezzar as god.

Babylonian religion considered the king as god on earth. The daily ritual consumption of meat and wine was therefore not only providing nourishment but aimed more specifically at making those involved to be loyal to the king. The Hebrew expression in Daniel 1:5 rendered literally as "they shall stand before the king" alludes to this function. It is a technical expression for those consecrated to religious service. In 2 Chronicles 29:11 it describes the function of the Levite. Chaldean education not only sought to indoctrinate the Hebrews but also threatened them in their most personal habits, so as to convert them to the cult of Nebuchadnezzar. And to symbolize this transfer of authority, they renamed the captives:

◆ Daniel, in Hebrew "God is my judge," they converted to Belteshazzar, signifying "may Bel [another name for Marduk, the principal Babylonian divinity] preserve his life."

◆ Hananiah, meaning "grace of God," became Shadrach, "order of Aku" (the Sumerian god of the moon).

◆ Mishael, "who is like God," the officials changed to Meshach, "who is like Aku."

◆ Azariah, whose name signified *"YHWH has helped,"* acquired the name Abednego, "servant of Nego" (a form of "Nabu," god of wisdom).

III. The Resistance (Dan. 1:8-16)

The three captives, especially Daniel, quickly reacted to the new program. Already the renditions of the Babylonian names in the book of Daniel allude to this. When compared to the names catalogued in secular documents, one can observe that in the biblical text the divine element has systematically been deformed.

Instead of Belshazzar, Daniel is named Belteshazzar (with a "t") so that the name of the god Bel has become Belt.

Instead of Shada Aku, Hananiah is called Shadrach. The name of the god Aku has been reduced to the Hebrew letter "k."

Instead of Mushallim-Marduk, Mishael carries the name Meshach. The name of the god Marduk is here also abridged to the Hebrew letter "k."

And instead of Ardi-Nabu, Azariah acquires the name

Abednego. Abed is the Hebrew translation of the Babylonian term *ardi,* "servant." As for the name of the god Nabu, it has been deformed into Nego (the *beth* has been replaced by the *gimmel,* the following letter in the Hebrew alphabet).

Thus, the names of the Babylonian gods lose their own identity. Through such linguistic slight of hand the author of the book of Daniel, as well as the bearers of the names themselves, expresses resistance to what was happening.

But their determination surpasses words and extends curiously to diet. The text uses the same Hebrew verb, *sam,* to refer to Daniel's resolution ("resolved," verse 8) and to the giving of new names ("gave," verse 7) by the chief of eunuchs. Through these echoes, the author intends to show that Daniel was directly responding to the king's attempt to force him into his Babylonian culture. To preserve his identity, the exile chooses to eat and drink differently. He asks for vegetables and water.

Beyond the "healthy choice" issue, the concern is essentially religious, something already hinted at in the text by Daniel's desire to "not be soiled" (see verse 8)—religious language found in the Levitical context of prohibited foods (Lev. 11). Daniel shares the same concern as any Jew in exile: kosher food. Yet there is more here. The phrase that Daniel uses to designate the menu he wishes to have is a literal quotation from the text of Creation. The same Hebrew words appear with the same associations: "vegetables,"[5] "given," "to be eaten" (see Gen. 1:29). In reformulating the same expression, Daniel is affirming that his God is the Creator and not the king. Thus his motivation is the same as the one implied in the Levitical laws of kosher: his faith in the Creator. Indeed, the dietary laws of clean and unclean meats also appear in the book of Leviticus in a way intended to remind the reader of the event of Creation in Genesis 1.[6] Because Daniel cannot control his food sources, he wisely then chooses to be vegetarian, the safest way to keep kosher and also the most explicit testimony of his faith in the God of Creation. By doing so, Daniel speaks a more universal language designed to reach the Gentiles who observe him at the table: his God is the God of Creation and therefore also their God.

But beyond his witnessing concern and his desire to remain faithful, Daniel's behavior contains an important lesson regarding the too often ignored connection between faith and existence. His religion does not limit itself to spiritual beliefs or to abstractions, but implies also the concrete level of existence. Daniel teaches us that faith involves both the soul and the life of the body. That religion concerns itself with eating can disconcert mind-sets influenced by Platonistic dualism. It remains nonetheless a biblical concern. The first test humans faced involved a dietary aspect. Adam and Eve determined their destiny and consequently that of humanity on the basis of a very simple eating choice (Gen. 3). Later, the Levitical laws on clean and unclean meats developed this same principle by establishing a link between food and holiness (Lev. 11:44, 45). Priests abstained from alcoholic beverages so as better to distinguish that which was sacred and that which was not (Lev. 10:8-11). In the desert the Israelites learned the same lesson. From falling quails to sprouting manna, such events had a religious aspect. Daniel was no innovator. His religious concern with diet had its roots in biblical tradition.

One must, however, observe that Daniel remains profoundly human. He is not an ascetic—far from it. In fact, the young Hebrews are handsome and their faces show no despondency, as the royal official thought they would (Dan. 1:10). It takes just 10 days[7] to provide proof that avoiding meat and wine does not prevent anyone from enjoying life. We must also note Daniel's behavior toward the king's official. His religious convictions and his ideal of sanctity do not make him arrogant. On the contrary, Daniel approaches his superior in humility and asks for "permission" (verse 8). He even maintains with him a relationship of friendship and respect (verse 9). His attitude contains an important lesson for all those obsessed by a desire for holiness. Holiness does not exclude humanity, but rather implies it. To drape oneself in the starched mantle of justice is not holiness nor is detachment from reality or the enjoyment of life. It is a distorted idea of holiness too long advocated by somber and emaciated "saints." Ignoring good food and laughter, they have rendered religion intolerable to the rest of us. In reaction there have appeared humanistic movements of all sorts with their slogans of love and fraternity. Somber saints have made the law of God suspect. Abraham Heschel declares that the secret to a godly life lies in being both "holy and human."[8] Daniel is a pleasant fellow who enjoys the reality of life while at the same time he refuses to compromise.

IV. The Liberation (Dan. 1:17–21)

And finally God intervenes. Until then He seemed absent. The text last mentioned God in the context of the captivity. The conclusion also mentions God, but this time in a positive sense. In the introduction God had "given" the Temple utensils to the king. Now He "gives" to the four young men science, intelligence, and wisdom (verse 17). The use of the same verb *(ntn)* highlights the symmetry of the two situations and reminds the reader of the existence of providence. The notion of God frames the chapter, alluding to His implicit presence and to His directing the course of events. It is He who "gives." If the Hebrew captives developed as they did, it is not a direct effect of intensive training, but the result of grace from above. One might, however, be tempted to derive from the text a relation of cause and effect between the 10 days and their resulting state of well-being. The passage repeats the number 10 as though the extent of their wisdom were proportional to their effort of 10 days. But that is really not the case. Daniel did not absorb this food as a "wonder drug," or use the ideal diet as a means to spiritual perfection, but as a sign of his faith in his God. In fact, Daniel and his companions took a risk, the risk of faith—and that is what saved them. To health and physical grace God added wisdom, intelligence, and science. They recognized the whole as a divine gift.

To supplement the lesson of grace, the text throws some light on human nature itself. Spiritual dimensions go hand in hand with intellectual and physical qualities. The human being, according to Daniel, is not a combination of soul and body, but must be considered as a whole, another revolutionary thought. Society often judges the person of faith as intellectually weak, and science does not easily accommodate itself with simplistic biblical explanations. On the other hand, we often expect health and beauty among people of little brainpower. One has difficulty imagining a man with pumped-up muscles deep in thought or involved in spiritual meditation. Daniel teaches us, however, that intelligence and physical development do not clash. The harmonious reunion of all the faculties is an ideal we need to seek. Not that we should now become obsessed by perfection and join some elite, but that we should give some thought to all the dimensions of the human being. Grace touches all of life. We are not the sole result of our actions, but rather the product of a gift, a grace from God. God meets Hebrew captives where they are and gives them happiness and success in the very heart of their misery.

But God's action does not stop there. Beyond their present exile, God prepares for them a salvation both of historical dimensions and of cosmic repercussions. The conclusion of the first chapter alludes to this through its mention of Cyrus, the king associated in the Bible with the return from exile and Israel's salvation (2 Chron. 36:21-23), and to the divine response to prayers and prophetic predictions (Isa. 45:1-13).

STRUCTURE OF DANIEL 1

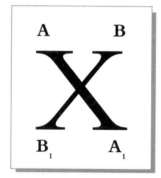

A Deportation: verses 1, 2

a) A date: 3rd year of Jehoiakim

b) Babylon overcomes Jerusalem

c) The Lord "gives" *(ntn)*

B Alienation: verses 3-7

a) The food appointed (allusion to the Creator, cf. Jonah 2:1; 4:6, 7)

b) A time: 3 years, motif of the end

c) Names "given" *(sam)*

B₁ Resistance: verses 8-16

a) Daniel "purposed" *(sam)*

b) The food requested (allusion to Creator, cf. Gen 1:29)

c) A time: 10 days, motif of the end

A₁ Liberation: verses 17-21

a) Hebrews overcome Babylon

b) God "gives" *(ntn)*

c) A date: 1st year of Cyrus

---

[1] Scholars have established the date not only on the basis of biblical chronology but also according to the astronomical cycles mentioned by the Babylonian chronicles that dated the king's reigns according to moon eclipses and conjunctions of planets.

[2] The list of requirements implies that the young men were between 16 and 18 years old. Moreover, Scripture uses the same term, *yeled*, of Joseph, who is about 18 years old when deported (Gen. 37:2, 30; see also 39:21-23).

[3] See *Antiquities* 10. 186; see also Talmud *b. Sanhedrin* 93b.

[4] The word *saris*, translated by most versions as "eunuch" (see the New King James Version; see also the Septuagint), implies that the person underwent castration. The original meaning of the word probably took on the more general connotation of a government official. It seems, however, that they were indeed eunuchs in the original sense of the term, as suggested by Assyrian depictions of court life that portray such officers as beardless.

[5] The Hebrew term used here for "vegetables" derives from *zera,* meaning seed and implying everything that grows on the face of the earth, including grains, fruits, and vegetables.

[6] The text of Leviticus 11 as it records these laws uses the same technical words and stylistic expressions (beasts of the earth, creeping animals, after its kind, etc.). Furthermore, the listing of the animals follows the same sequence as in Genesis 1:24-26 (the sixth day of Creation). After the creation of the animals of the earth (Lev. 11:2-8; cf. Gen. 1:24, 25), the creation of man is related successively to that of water animals (Lev. 11:9-12; cf. Gen. 1:26), that of the animals of the air (Lev. 11:13-23; cf. Gen. 1:26), and that of land animals, including reptiles (Lev. 11:24-43; cf. Gen. 1:26). Last, in Leviticus 11, as in Genesis 1:24-26, the relationship between humans and animals has its counterpart in the relationship between humans and God. Genesis 1:26 associates the duty of domination over the animals with the fact that God created humans in His image. Likewise Leviticus 11 links the duty to distinguish between clean and unclean meats with the fact that human holiness reflects divine holiness: "be holy, because I am holy" (Lev. 11:44, 45).

[7] In the Bible the number 10 symbolizes a minimum amount for something (Gen. 18:32; Amos 5:3; 6:9). We should also add that Hebrew represents 10 by the smallest letter of the alphabet, *yod.* In a temporal context, it symbolizes a time span in which we find ourselves put to the test. A countdown of 10 days exists also between the Feast of Trumpets and the Day of Atonement, serving as a time of preparation and testing.

[8] Abraham Heschel, *God in Search of Man* (New York: 1955), p. 238.

CHAPTER 2

THE GIANT
AND THE MOUNTAIN

Three years have passed since the arrival of the captives from Jerusalem.[1] We are in 603 B.C.E.—where we left off in the preceding chapter (Dan. 1:18, 19). Daniel and his companions have just graduated from the Babylonian schools and have successfully passed the king's examination. From now on they belong to the class of the Chaldeans. There then occurs an event of shattering repercussions. Nebuchadnezzar finds himself gripped by a vision that plunges him, and the whole kingdom with him, into turmoil. Nowadays we might trace the significance of such a dream back to the deeper layers of the unconscious, to childhood days, or perhaps even as resulting from the hearty meal indulged in the night before. Back then, however, particularly in Babylon, society welcomed dreams as divine messages and sometimes compiled them in "books of dreams." The people went so far as to spend the night in a temple in order to receive divine messages. Thus the king's emotion hardly surprises us. "His mind was troubled" (Dan. 2:1). The verb *titpaem* used here to express the king's feelings derives from a root that means "the beating of footsteps," close to what the sound of the king's heart might have been. Nebuchadnezzar is interested in not only the dream's meaning but also its content. "My heart beats for the knowledge of this dream" (verse 3, literal trans.).

24

I. The Elusive Dream

The Babylonian king remembers having dreamed something and senses its importance, but he has forgotten the content. Here is a bizarre paradox. Indeed, if Nebuchadnezzar cannot remember the content, how can he perceive its significance? By the fact that the dream has repeated itself several times. The word "dreams" appears in the plural (verse 1). This recurrence of the same dream is strange, and the very fact that he keeps forgetting it is enough to alert the king to its extraordinary character. But there remains yet another question: If Nebuchadnezzar dreamed several times, and if he has understood its importance, how is it that he came to forget the dream?

The first explanation we shall venture is a psychological one: the king blanked his dream precisely because he felt overwhelmed by it. This implies that the king comprehended the divine message, and that, terrified, he repressed the vision's content to escape a reality he felt was threatening. Daniel himself will later confirm this first level of explanation when he announces to Nebuchadnezzar that the dream came to the king "so that you . . . may understand what went through your mind" (verse 30). But there is yet another reason, this time belonging to the realm of the supernatural. God Himself may have originated the amnesia. Babylon considered the act of forgetting a dream as already a sign that it had a divine source: "If a man forgets his dream, this signifies that his god is angry at him."[2] The Chaldeans themselves allude to this. "There is not a man on earth who can do what the king asks!" (verse 10), and they even admit: "except the gods, and they do not live among men" (verse 11). Indeed, only a revelation from above will elucidate their ruler's dream. Daniel himself points this out to the king: "No wise man, enchanter, magician or diviner can explain to the king the mystery he has asked about, but there is a God in heaven who reveals mysteries" (verses 27, 28). The very fact that the king forgot the dream offers proof of its divine origin. It is not just a subjective fantasy. The king's memory lapse thus becomes a criterion of objectivity, a test, permitting him to judge the competence of the dream's interpreters: "So then, tell me the dream, and I will know that you can interpret it for me" (verse 9). The king provides no hint to put them on the right track. Nebuchadnezzar is not content with a simple astrologer's guess. He wants to know the only possible and true explanation of his dream. Truth is also unique and specific. In comparison to revelation, all other claims to truths are then "misleading and wicked things" (verse 9), a means "to gain time" (verse 8). Nebuchadnezzar has understood this, and in a flash of lucidity, suddenly realizes that the soothsayers have deceived him. The king's anguish then turns to wrath. Actually, it is because the king is afraid that he threatens to kill. Violence and anger often express anguish and fear.

The disproportionate character of his punishment confirms such a diagnosis: "I will have you cut into pieces and your houses turned into piles of rubble" (verse 5). Nebuchadnezzar is not joking, and no one dare ignore his threats. The Assyrians and Babylonians were well known in antiquity for their cruelty. Cutting up the bodies of enemies and burning their houses was common practice in ancient Mesopotamia. Everyone must take the wrath of the king seriously. It will spare no one. Since Chaldeans are charlatans and liars, the king will have all the wise men executed (verse 14). All, including Daniel.

II. Prayer for a Secret

Daniel replies to the king's fury "with wisdom and tact" (verse 14). The two opposite reactions characterize king and prophet throughout the book. Withdrawing then with his friends, Daniel prays to the "God of heaven concerning this mystery" (verse 18). *The first prayer of the book of Daniel,* it is not a formula dictated by the habit of daily worship nor by automatic ritual. The prophet did not craft it just to delight a congregation. Neither does it spring from the quasi-superstitious notion that the more one embellishes a prayer, the more chance it has to reach God's throne. No, rather it is a cry of supplication, tense and hoarse. Eminent death awaits Daniel and his companions.

His prayer expects an answer. He does not pray out of obligation, but to receive a divine response. It is wrong to reduce prayer to a simple exercise of piety that somehow meets a person's psychological and other basic needs. Prayer is essentially an encounter with a real Person, a Person external to ourselves. We speak to a God who will answer.

And indeed, the God of heaven responds. "During the night the mystery was revealed to Daniel in a vision" (verse 19). The prophet recognizes the mechanism behind the revelation. He does not gain access to divine secrets through practicing special techniques, or because of superior intellectual or literary skill. "This mystery has been revealed to me, not because I have greater wisdom than other living men" (verse 30). Daniel understands that answer to prayer does not depend on who is praying—the passage also mentions the prayer of his companions (verse 18)—or on the person's worth.

The process has an up-down orientation to it, rather than a down-up one. Herein lies the principal difference between Daniel's prayer and the magic of the Chaldeans. For the Chaldeans it all occurs below, on the technical level, thus their insistence to know the dream's content. Access to the divine realms is to them inconceivable, as the gods "do not live among men" (verse 11). Daniel, on the other hand, does not need the dream's data to elucidate it, for his God "reveals mysteries" (verse 28). It is interesting to note that the expression "God of heaven" is a key phrase throughout the book and generally associated with the word "secret." But the Chaldeans understand it in the negative sense as secrets locked up in the divine spheres while Daniel approaches it in a positive sense as secrets revealed by the God in heaven. Each time this association appears, it emphasizes God's involvement in history (Dan. 2:27-30, 44, 45; 4:36; 5:23, 24). The God of Daniel, as opposed to the one of the Chaldeans, does not remain secluded or indifferent to human events. Rather, the God of heaven not only controls history but also reveals secrets. He is the God who descends and communicates with people.

His request granted, Daniel now renders thanks. The prophet blesses the God of heaven, for "wisdom and power are his" (Dan. 2:20). But Daniel also blesses Him because He has come down and has given that which was inherently His: "You have given me wisdom and power, you have made known to me what we asked of you" (verse 23; cf. verse 21). This echo of divine attributes that God presents as gifts to humanity reminds us of Daniel's dependency on God. In giving thanks, Daniel recognizes that he now holds the king's secret; that his prayer was not in vain. But the revelation is also a grace of God, something given independently of Daniel's efforts. In fact, the divine favor is not ultimately meant for him. Even though revealing the meaning of the dream saves the prophet's life, that is of secondary importance and does not even come up in his prayer of thankfulness. God's answer encompasses more than just the prophet's fate. What is important is the destiny of the world—"what will happen in days to come" (verse 28)—and the salvation of the king—so "that you . . . may understand what went through your mind" (verse 30). In this sense, Daniel's prayer is a true prayer, for it has no personal aim but is offered in service to God, to humanity, and to history. Instead of calling to God from below, the prayer is offered to God that His will may be done. It is essentially a deep longing for God's kingdom. Behind the desire to know the king's secret lies a deeper yearning for God's reign here on earth. Thus we must understand Nebuchadnezzar's prophetic dream announcing God's kingdom as a direct answer to Daniel's prayer.

III. Dream of Kingdoms

The first words already hint at the prophetic nature of the king's dream. The verb *hzh,* translated as "to look," is the technical term in the Bible to designate the prophetic vision (Isa. 1:1; 2:1; 13:1; Amos 1:1; Micah 1:1; Hab. 1:1; Eze. 13:6; Dan. 8:13, 15, 26, etc.). In our passage the verb outlines two stages in the dream. The first "you looked" (Dan. 2:31) introduces a statue of giant proportions cast from four metals degrading in value from the head of gold to the feet of iron and clay. The second "you looked" (verse 34) introduces the destruction of the statue by a cut-out stone that becomes a huge mountain filling the whole earth (verse 35).

The dream looks beyond Nebuchadnezzar and his kingdom, thus extending from the present to the future until the end. Today it is possible, in retrospect, to follow the prophet's gaze through history. We can develop the explanation of the dream in parallel with the unrolling of history, always checking the prophet's testimony against historical reality.

The language of the vision is actually quite explicit for the king. Most likely the astrologers would have been able to decipher it once they knew its contents. Ancient Middle Eastern culture often used the statue of a human being to represent the world's destiny. Egyptian astrologers particularly employed it.[3] Moreover, the number 4 was significant, since the ancients used it to symbolize the terrestrial dimension (Dan. 7:2; 11:4; Eze. 37:9; Rev. 7:1; 2:8).[4] The dream suggests two orders: the terrestrial order of the metals (Dan. 2:31-33, in 41 Hebrew words) and the order of the stone (verses 34, 35, in 49 words). The only question now concerns the meaning of the four metals and of the detached stone that engulfs the whole space formerly taken by the metals.

Daniel's explanation confirms and develops all this.

1. The Statue

The head of gold. Nebuchadnezzar did not need Daniel's help to understand that the head of gold represented his own kingdom. The listing of the metals in descending order from head to toe, and the successive events described in the destructive process of the stone, hint at a chronological progression. It was then possible for the king to deduce that the head represented the first stage, especially since the word "head" in Hebrew and in Aramaic means "beginning" or "first." Moreover, gold was the most popular metal in Babylon. Upon his arrival in Babylon, the Greek historian Herodotus could not but marvel at the lavish use of gold in temples and palace construction. Walls, statues, and other objects of gold testified to Babylon's splendor and glory (Herodotus 1. 181, 183; 3. 1-7). The prophet Jeremiah compared Babylon to a golden cup (Jer. 51:7), an interpretation Daniel now elaborates: "You, O king, are the king of kings. The God of heaven has given you dominion and power and might and glory; in your hands he has placed mankind and the beasts of the field and the birds of the air. Wherever they live, he has made you ruler over them all. You are that head of gold" (Dan. 2:37, 38).

The title "king of kings" and the dominion given over all living things indicate Babylon's superiority over the others. "King of kings" was, of course, also the official title of the king at the court of Babylon, and Ezekiel 26:7 specifically applies it to Nebuchadnezzar. The empire called Babylonian kings by this name (in Akkadian: *shar sharrani,* "king of kings") because they controlled regional principalities and their respective kinglets. But in the mouth of Daniel the title implies more than local kingship. His seat in the head of gold establishes Nebuchadnezzar as the epoch's supreme ruler. Moreover, the fact that God gives him domination over all living things reminds one of Adam's responsibility worded in the same language in Genesis 1:28. The passage here identifies Nebuchadnezzar as the first man; for like Adam, he is king over the earth, and like Adam, he introduces history. At the same time, however, the vision reminds Nebuchadnezzar of his dependence upon God. The power he possesses implies the responsibility to administer and protect, but it is something that comes only as a gift and is not inherent in him. Despite the intoxication of power he is to remember this, lest he forget his own limitations and follow in the footsteps of ancient Babel (Gen. 11:1-9). The prophecy encompasses, however, more than just Nebuchadnezzar's person. The word "king" often serves in Scripture as a synonym of "kingdom": "After you, another kingdom will rise" (Dan. 2:39; see also verse 44; Dan. 7:17). The "head of gold," the first kingdom, represents then the kingdom of Babylon from the beginning of the reign of Nebuchadnezzar in 605 B.C.E. to its fall in 539 B.C.E.

The chest and arms of silver. After Babylon comes another empire, inferior to its predecessor, as the vision implicitly indicates through the lesser value of silver, and as Daniel also explicitly states: "Another kingdom will rise, inferior to yours" (Dan. 2:39). The succeeding kingdom is that of the Medes and the Persians. But the vision does not solely allude to the Persian kingdom, as some commentators have suggested, because the Persian kingdom was contemporary with the Babylonian kingdom and not its successor. In fact, the kingdom of the Medes fell under Persian domination after a battle between Cyrus of Persia and Astyages, king of the Medes, in 550 B.C.E. Moreover, Cyrus was of Median descent, being through his mother's lineage the grandson of King Astyages, whom he dethroned and defeated. According to Herodotus (1. 206), Tomyris, queen of the Massagetae, refers to Cyrus as "King of the

Medes." Against this historical background, one understands better why Scripture refers to the kingdom as that of the "Medes and the Persians." Daniel uses the same expression several times to describe the kingdom following Babylon (Dan. 5:28; 6:8; 8:20). A century later the book of Esther confirms this (Esther 1:3). In spite of its larger geographical scope, the kingdom of the Medes and the Persians was culturally inferior to Babylon. In fact, Median and Persian conquerors adopted Babylonian civilization, by far the most complex and advanced until then.

The reference to silver alludes to a major characteristic of the next kingdom. Persians used silver in their taxation system. According to Herodotus (3. 89-95), the satraps had to pay the tribute imposed on them with silver. Only the more affluent Indian satraps had to pay their dues with gold. And even then, the authorities measured it in terms of silver. Clearly, the standard monetary value for the Persians of the time was silver. On a broader level, silver served as a characteristic for this kingdom in that it alluded to its wealth, wealth that guaranteed the Persian kings their power (Dan. 11:2). Indeed, history remembers them as the "rich and powerful" of the era, as Herodotus testifies about Darius as "someone making profit from all" (Herodotus 3. 89). The supremacy of the Medo-Persian kingdom lasted from 539 B.C.E., the fall of Babylon, to 331 B.C.E., the defeat of the last Persian king, Darius III, by the Greco-Macedonian armies.

The belly and thighs of bronze. Bronze stands for the next kingdom. It symbolizes the conquering power of Greece. The metal was a Greek specialty. The prophet Ezekiel refers to bronze as the principal means of exchange among the Greeks (Eze. 27:13).[5] The Greek army especially employed bronze in their armor, helmets, shields, and even their weapons. We are told that when the Egyptian pharaoh Psammetic the First consulted the oracle of Laton inquiring of a way to avenge himself against his Persian foes, the reply said that "revenge would come from the sea in the hands of the men of bronze." The Egyptian monarch regarded the answer with some skepticism until the appearance one morning of shipwrecked Greek armies in their shiny bronze armor on the Egyptian shores. Seeing in them the fulfillment of the oracle, King Psammetic allied himself with them against his enemies (Herodotus 2. 153, 154).

In addition to a connotation of decadence after following gold and silver, bronze also implied the idea of conquest. The bronze armor of the Greek soldiers sharply contrasted with the simple woven gowns worn by Median and Persian soldiers (Herodotus 7. 61, 62).

We now understand better the implications behind this kingdom of bronze that is to "rule over the whole earth" (Dan. 2:39). History confirms the divine prophecy. Sweeping over Phoenicia, Palestine, and Egypt, the armies of Alexander the Great stretched the boundaries of the kingdom of Greece as far as India and Persia. Not only did Alexander take the title of "King of Persia" as the successor of the Medo-Persian kings, but he established himself as master of the world. And it was not only in a military sense. Greek culture now flourished in the most remote corners of the empire. Aware that such a vast empire could easily disintegrate, Alexander sought to gain the trust of its inhabitants by assimilating his soldiers into the native population, even encouraging intermarriage. He gave the example by wedding a Persian princess. From then on, Greek language and culture spread everywhere and still influences civilization to this day. Greek hegemony would last from 331 B.C.E., date of the victory of Alexander against the Persians, to 168 B.C.E., when Rome took Macedonia over. The empire annexed it in 142 B.C.E.

The legs of iron. After the age of bronze, the prophetic dream foretells a period of iron. Bronze was to the Greeks as iron was to the Romans. Latin poets testify of this transition. Virgil describes armies of old as being equipped in bronze: "Bronze flashes on their shields, flashes with bronze their sword."[6] Likewise, Lucretius contrasts bronze with that of iron: "The use of bronze was known before iron. . . . With bronze men tilled the soil . . . with bronze they stirred up the waves of war."[7]

Such passages in Latin literature testify that the transition of bronze to iron paralleled that of the Greek to the Roman Empire. Considering historical reality, the Roman army is indeed one of iron with its iron sword, shield, armor, helmet, and particularly its *pilum,* an iron spear that could also serve as a javelin. But the explanation of Daniel aims at more than the metal itself. Iron also symbolizes "strength" (verse 41) and a behavior that "breaks and smashes everything . . . to pieces" (verse 40).

The strength of the Roman Empire also lay in its means of governing. Not content just to expand its conquests even farther than those of its predecessors, Rome also developed a highly advanced form of politics. Besides being the first republic in history, it had a sophisticated administrative system permitting control from afar of even the most diverse peoples. Such government maintained the empire's unity and safeguarded world peace, then known as the *Pax Romana*. The Roman naturalist poet Pliny the Elder (C.E. 23-79) depicted it, and justly so, as "the infinite greatness of the Roman peace." During the time of the emperor Vespasian, he added, "The power of Rome has enabled the unity of Rome; all should recognize her contribution in facilitating relations between different ethnic groups, permitting them to commonly benefit from the *Pax Romana.*"[8]

With its iron army and its iron grip in leadership issues, one understands better the text's observation that Rome "smashes everything" (verse 40). We remember the crushing victories of the Roman army; of Julius Caesar's historical saying: *"Veni, vidi, vici* ["I came, I saw, I vanquished"]." But beyond these successes, one recalls especially the way Caesar treated those who dared resist. The policy of reprisals inflicted on ancient Gaul that resulted in the burning of entire villages, the suppression of the Druids, the destruction of Carthage, and the siege of Jerusalem are all eloquent examples of the crushing power of Rome.

Longevity is also a sign of strength. Roman rule lasted 500 years, far longer than any of its predecessors. Rome would then succumb to barbarian invasions. Odoacer, a Germanic chief, dethroned the last emperor in 476.

The feet of iron and clay. Judging from the length of it—more than half of the passage (verses 41-43)—the events here described seem to have been of primary interest to the prophet. The text does not describe this new kingdom as being separate from the one of iron preceding it. Rather, it still belongs to the fourth kingdom, as the traces of iron indicate.

But a new element, that of clay, interpenetrates the old. This strange association takes on three levels of meaning:

1. It "will be a divided kingdom" (verse 41). The relationship here is a negative one. The association of clay and iron implies division, a fact particularly significant, since it occurs right after a period characterized by its unity. A retrospective look at history confirms this. Indeed, since the fall of Rome the region of the former empire has yet to achieve unity; and if we are to believe the prophet, it will never do so.

2. "This kingdom will be partly strong and partly brittle" (verse 42). The passage regards the iron and clay as distinct entities. Iron is to strength as clay is to weakness. The kingdom, now divided, becomes a heterogeneous composition of weak and strong elements. The territory of the former Roman Empire is a collection of both strong and weak, rich and poor nations.

But clay and iron mean more than "strong and weak." In the preceding kingdoms, each of the elements—gold, silver, bronze, and iron—had a representative function. In this context, it becomes likely that the element of clay should also have its own particular symbolic role. Let us note also that from metal to clay the transition is more than abrupt. Up until now the metals represented political powers. Clay represents, then, a power of an essentially different nature. Moreover, Daniel specifies that this clay is "potter's clay" (verse 41, NKJV). Scripture uses the image of clay, especially potter's clay, in the context of Creation: "Yet, O Lord, you are our Father. We are the clay, you are the potter; we are all the work of your hand" (Isa. 64:8).

When the Bible employs the word "clay," it is always in association with the word "potter," and always evokes the human person in a relationship of dependence upon the Creator.[9] The reference to clay thus has a strong religious connotation. We have good reasons to believe that the clay at the base of the statue represents a different power of a religious nature, though associated with the political power symbolized by iron.

On a historical level, this means that following the dissolution of the Roman Empire a new power would take over, a religious one, though related more or less to the political power of Rome. This politico-religious power should even be alive today, since the text has it surviving until the time of the end.

The ancient rabbis have hotly debated the mysterious identity of this power, though they have reached a consensus on the four kingdoms. Most all agree that the latter refer respectively to Babylon, Greece, (Medo-) Persia, and Rome. According to the traditional sages and to most Jewish commentators after them, the fourth kingdom (iron and iron/clay) is undoubtedly Rome and more precisely its associate, Edom. In Jewish tradition, Edom represents the bloody enemy of Israel who is yet its brother.

No wonder, then, that for most Jewish commentators this strange politico-religious power is none other than Christianity, the sister religion of Judaism. Adopted by the Roman Empire, the orphan religion would later become the state religion and would soon oppress the Jewish people. From a Jewish perspective, the church fits perfectly prophecy's portrayal. The ArtScroll commentary on Daniel sums up this perspective:

"According to commentators, Rome, in the heavenly vision (7:8) seen by Daniel and explained by the angel undergoes a metamorphosis from the secular power of the old empire into the religious power, Christianity. The powerless orphan adopted by the mighty empire, originally by Emperor Constantine I and later by his successors, grew up to utilize its unique position as state religion of the great empire and moved on to a period of unprecedented growth. Its power, whether temporal or spiritual, eclipses that of kingdoms and empires. Thus throughout our exile, the fourth kingdom is represented by the Christian church, conceived of, despite all its diverse forms, as one unit."[10]

3. "So the people will be a mixture" (Dan. 2:43). The relationship is now a positive one alluding to a tentative alliance between the two elements. Then, "in the time of those kings, the God of heaven will set up a kingdom" (verse 44).

Also, this period is the only one in the vision during which any action takes place. Up to now, the inspired explanations focused on a state of being or a quality: "divided" (verse 41), "strong" and "weak" (verse 42, TEV). Whereas the two characteristics describe a state that lasts until the end, the action now described takes place *at* the end of times.

For the first time, the word is in the plural and designates several "kings" (verse 44). Before, the kingdom had been one in spite of its divisions (verse 41) and its weak and strong parts (verse 42). The vision depicts a hectic end-time rush to conclude alliances that never really work out. One cannot help thinking of the episode of Babel. Already verse 41 alludes to the tower of Babel in the use of the root *plg* (divided). The biblical tradition generally links this root, from which comes the name *Peleg,* to the tower of Babel event: "Because in his time the earth was divided," *palag* (Gen. 10:25; 1 Chron. 1:19). The prophecy of Daniel thus foretells an event related to that of the tower of Babel. In the Genesis story God descends from heaven at the moment when, in fear of being destroyed, the people of the earth unite to erect a tower and give themselves a name (Gen. 11:4). Likewise, God intervenes at the end of time when the powers of the world, also because of their fear of destruction, attempt to unite by "human alliances."

If a renewed concern for unity does characterize the end-times, it is strangely relevant today. Never in human history have there been so many worldwide attempts at unity. It is the distinctive feature of our modern politics. For the first time, the powers of the earth feel the need to merge or come together, thus encouraging alliances on all levels: political ones such as NATO, OAU, UN, etc.; economical coalitions such as the Common Market, the EEC, the OPEC, etc.; and even religious alliances such as the ecumenical movement, and politico-religious ones like the right-wing ideologies.

But recently humanity has been concocting a more audacious alliance. Going beyond mere continental or ideological alliances since the fall of Communism, world powers now dare to dream of global politics: the New World Order.

Could it be that the prophecy is referring to our time?

2. The Stone

We now enter the most important part of the vision. It occupies the largest portion of the king's dream and seems to be the point toward which everything appears to converge. It is the second part of the dream, the explanation of which follows the same two-part structure as the exposition (see above). Earlier Daniel had introduced his explanation with a reference to the "God of heaven" who gives dominion (Dan. 2:37). Likewise, the prophet begins this second part with a comment about the "God of heaven" who now sets up a kingdom (verse 44). This parallel on the introductory levels implicitly contrasts the two parts of the dream. In the first part, the kingdoms are given to humanity, while in the second part the "God of heaven" sets up the kingdom and it remains in His control. In fact, the second kingdom is nothing like the first, opposing it on all levels.

The material. We can contrast the unity of the stone with the diversity of the statue's metals. The second order (depicted in the second part of the dream) comprises only one kingdom, whereas the first consists of several. Scripture uses the imagery of stone in the context of an alliance made with God: to build the altar (Ex. 20:24), the monument (Deut. 27:4), and the Temple (1 Kings 6:7), and as a tablet for engraving the commandments in the alliance between God and Israel (Ex. 24:12). This explains the commandment forbidding the use of tools on stone (Ex. 20:25), for it could easily degenerate into the fabrication of idols (Lev. 26:1). The stone in its brute form, as a material for construction, came to symbolize the divine dimension, and by extension God Himself and the Messiah (Ps. 118:22; Isa. 28:16; Zach. 3:9; Acts 4:11).

On the other hand, biblical imagery often associates metals with the manufacture of idols and implies a religion of human inspiration. The book of Daniel always relates metals with the idolatrous act, especially those forming the statue (Dan. 3:5; 5:4, 23). The stone symbolizes the kingdom of God, while the metals represent human kingdoms. As for the clay, it supposedly refers to the religious dimension, but in its association with iron it loses its biblical prerogatives and takes the form of idolatrous acts.

Its origins. The intrusion of the stone cut out "but not by human hands" (Dan. 2:34, 45), contrasts with the static character of the metals. The kingdom of the stone is different from the kingdoms of the statue in that the God of heaven sets it up (verse 44). It is from above. In his explanation, Daniel sees the stone as a "mountain" (verse 45). Babylonian thought regarded "the mountain" as the domicile of the great gods, especially Enlil, the supreme deity who lived in the heavens. According to Babylonian beliefs, this mountain touched the sky and supported the heavenly residence of the supreme god. For Nebuchadnezzar, the allusion to a "huge mountain" (verse 35) is then very clear: the stone, "cut out of a mountain" (verse 45) and thrown from the heavens, represents a kingdom of divine origin. For the Hebrew prophet, the mountain symbolizes Zion or Jerusalem (Dan. 9:16, 20; 11:45) and by extension the heavenly residence. Scripture often pictures the mountain of Zion, or Jerusalem for that matter, as being in the heavens. The language of Psalm 48:2 alludes to the mountain of Zion as situated in the "utmost heights" (literally: "the extremes of the Zaphon"), a technical expression designating the heavenly place of God (Isa. 14:13).

Moreover, the Aramaic word *tur,* or mountain, is the equivalent to the Hebrew word *tsur,* "rock." The Bible often uses it to symbolize God Himself. The stone is carved out of the rock and is consequently not only of divine origin, but of a divine nature. The two motifs—"rock" *(tsur)* and "stone" *(eben)*—are synonymous and represent God (Isa. 8:14).

Its nature. The vision opposes the stone to the statue by having it *thrown* against the latter. The verb "strike" employed in Daniel 2:35 suggests a struggle, a clash between the two orders. The kingdom set up by God is not an offshoot of human kingdoms. All the human kingdoms have been "broken to pieces" (verse 35), destroyed and completely crushed (verse 44), "without leaving a trace" (verse 35). The new kingdom has nothing to do with its predecessors, even the clay being destroyed along with the iron (verses 35, 45).

The essential difference lies in the fact that it comes from elsewhere: the stone carved out of the mountain changes back, its mission accomplished, to a "huge mountain" (verse 35). The coincidence between the origin and the outcome implicitly testifies to the kingdom's divine nature. Nothing of the old order remains.

Finally, the new kingdom "will itself endure forever" (verse 44). The earthly kingdoms were temporary, and all eventually collapsed.

The final kingdom, on the other hand, will last forever. The eternal defeats the ephemeral. We can appreciate the contrast between the two orders even on a spatial level. Gigantic as it was, the statue becomes dwarfed by the mountain that "filled the whole earth" (verse 35). The infinite overwhelms the finite.

The heavenly kingdom spreads over the whole earth and remains forever. Our rational minds find such a thing hard to imagine. We find ourselves tempted to follow a number of theologians and philosophers and "demythologize" the vision. The kingdom of heaven then takes on the more reasonable proportions of a church, a people, the enlightened self, and so on.

Jewish tradition views the final kingdom as representing all the hopes of Israel. It cannot be human but must be the kingdom of the Messiah. Rashi and Ibn Ezra, following ancient Jewish interpretation, regarded it as that of "King Messiah," *malkut melek hamashiah.*[11] Thus *Tanhuma,* commenting on "while you were watching" (verse 34), explains: "Reish Laqish said: 'It is the king Messiah.'"[12] On verse 35 Pirkey Eliezer identifies the "King || Messiah, who, in the future, will rule from one end of the world to the other."[13]

Daniel's argument with Nebuchadnezzar that the "interpretation is trustworthy" lies in the fact that the "dream is true" (verse 45). A *waw* links the two clauses, a conjunction of coordination that also functions as a conjunction of consequence. We may understand Daniel's last words as being "The dream is true," *therefore* "the interpretation is trustworthy." Proof beckons one to faith. The king understands the lesson and draws its implications for himself.

Prayer by transfer. Prayer is the only possible response. "Then King Nebuchadnezzar fell prostrate . . ." (verse 46). *This is the second prayer in the book of Daniel.* The king does not yet dare to address the God of heaven, a deity too distant, too strange, maybe too disturbing for him. Instead, the king carries his gesture of prayer to the feet of Daniel. It does not necessarily mean that the king mistakes Daniel for his God and that he intends to adore him. In the same way, according to the testimony of Flavius Josephus, Alexander the Great lies on the ground before the priest of Jerusalem, saying: "It was not before him that I prostrated myself but the God of whom he has the honour to be high priest."[14] Moreover, Nebuchadnezzar clearly recognizes God's sovereignty: "Your God is the God of gods" (verse 47). In so doing, he seems to submit himself to "the Lord of kings" (verse 47). But one must not be deceived by the sudden eloquence. The expressions used are quite ambiguous. "Lord of kings" was in fact another name for Marduk, the Babylonian deity of royalty, and for Nabu, a name borne by the king himself, "son of Marduk." The king's confession is at best dubious. The Babylonian ruler has not yet understood who God is. He speaks of the God of Daniel, but he winks to his own god: "Your God, Daniel, is mine; your power you owe to my god, my father." The king has not changed. His act of adoration is ambiguous.

That is why we find no happy ending. The king does not undergo the expected steps of repentance, but instead turns to Daniel. The Babylonian ruler shifts from a vertical response toward God Himself to a horizontal one toward Daniel. Nebuchadnezzar realizes Daniel's worthiness, but his appreciation stops there. The religion of Nebuchadnezzar does not go beyond the human person of Daniel.

His prayer is contaminated with the pride of a man who prefers his own religion and chooses his own idol over the true God. It is easier to prostrate oneself before a statue or even a human being than to do so before an invisible God. The proof given by Daniel did not have its full effect. Nebuchadnezzar now believes in God's existence, but he does not yet worship Him. He prefers to avoid a relationship with this unpredictable God of the future. God's plan for Nebuchadnezzar has so far failed.

It is not difficult to recognize the historical plausibility of Daniel's prophecy. We can easily identify the kingdoms of Babylon, the Medes and Persians, Greece, Rome, etc. And we may even be convinced that God sent the dream and join Nebuchadnezzar in admitting that He is the "revealer of mysteries" (verse 47). But when it comes to events beyond history, such as the nebulous kingdom of God, we would rather remain skeptical.

And yet the whole raison d'être of the prophetic dream was to convince us of its historicity down to the last events, including those concerning the kingdom of God. Nebuchadnezzar's dream could have restricted itself only to this last and apparently most important kingdom. But it prefers instead to meander across history, enabling us to verify step by step the validity of the prophecy. None of the statue's kingdoms are very important—they serve only as landmarks leading to the last prophecy concerning the divine kingdom. They also act as chronological markers, situating God's coming kingdom in time. The statue's four kingdoms teach us two things about God's kingdom: first, it is real and will actually manifest itself in history, just as the human kingdoms did. Second, the data of the prophecy allow us to conclude that we are in the time of the end, close to its appearance. Like Nebuchadnezzar, we base our belief on what we have already seen. Our awareness of history awakens and strengthens our faith in the God of the future.

STRUCTURE OF DANIEL 2

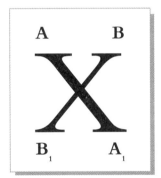

**A Nebuchadnezzar:
  forgotten dream (verses 1-13)**
a) three dialogues
   (Nebuchadnezzar—Chaldeans)
b) Nebuchadnezzar's command

B Daniel: prayer (verses 14-23)
a) three requests (Daniel/Arioch,
   King, God)
b) Daniel's prayer

B₁ (A₁) Daniel:
revealed dream (verses 24-45)

a) three dialogues

(Daniel ➜ Arioch ➜ King ➜

Daniel)

b) Daniel's explanation of the dream

I. The Exposition

1. "you were watching,"

verse 31 (image)

2. "you were watching,"

verse 34

(stone ➜ mountain)

II. The Interpretation

1. "the God of heaven has

given you a kingdom,"

verse 37 (image)

2. "the God of heaven has

set up a kingdom," verse

44 (mountain ➜ stone)

A₁ (B₁) Nebuchadnezzar:
prayer (verses 46-49)

a) three King's actions to Daniel

(prostrate, answered, promoted)

---

[1] The second year of Nebuchadnezzar (Dan. 2:1) corresponds, in fact, to the third year of his reign. Often the ancients omitted the year of succession to the throne so that the same event had different datings according to the system used (see, for example, 2 Kings 8:25 and 9:29; see also Dan. 11:1 and Jer. 28:1).

[2] See A. Leo Oppenheim, *Le rêve, son interprétation dans le Proche-Orient ancien* (Paris: 1959).

[3] André J. Festugière, *La Révélation d'Hermès Trismégiste* (Paris: 1950), vol. 1, pp. 92, 93.

[4] See the oracles of Persia and of Babylon in James B. Pritchard, ed., *The Ancient Near East. Supplementary Texts and Pictures Relating to the Old Testament* (Princeton: 1969), pp. 606, 607; see also the Greek poet Hesiod of the eighth century B.C.E. (*Works and Days* 109-180), and even the Latin poet Ovid (*Metamorphoses* 1. 89-414).

[5] The Hebrew text speaks of *Yavan,* the Hebrew word for "Greek." The word originally meant "pigeon" and probably alluded to the carrier pigeons kept on the Greek islands. From there the term came to designate the inhabitants of those islands (Felix M. Abel, *Géographie de la Palestine* [Paris: 1967], pp. 259, 260). Also, the word "Ionian," "Ionia" (from Ion, name of one of the sons of Helen), derives from the Hebrew *Yavan.*

[6] Virgil *Aeneid* 7. 742, 743.

[7] Lucretius *De Rerum Natura* 5. 1286-1294.

[8] André Alba, *Rome et le Moyen Age jusqu'en 1328* (Paris: 1964), p. 126.

[9] Isa. 29:16; 41:25; 45:9; Jer. 18:2; 19:1; Lam. 4:2; Rom. 9:21.

[10] Nosson Scherman and Meir Zlotowitz, eds., *Daniel,* ArtScroll Tanach Series (Brooklyn: Mesorah Pubns., 1979), p. 105.

[11] *Miqraoth Gdoloth.*

[12] *Tanhuma* Ex. 25:3, 4.

[13] Rabbi Eliezer, *Pirkê de Rabbi Eliezer,* trans. Gerald Friedlander (New York: 1971), p. 83.

[14] *Antiquities* 11. 333.

CHAPTER 3

FOOTSTEPS IN
THE FURNACE

Now we encounter more statues, but this time the dream does not derive from God but results from Nebuchadnezzar's own desires. Having understood that according to the dream of the statue his reign would hardly go beyond the head of the statue, Nebuchadnezzar decides to revise history. He orders the erection of the human statue that he saw in his dreams, employing the same term *tselem* used to designate the first statue (Dan. 3:1; cf. 2:31), whose purpose was to remind him of his limitations. But he reproduces it *entirely* in gold. Nebuchadnezzar wants a kingdom that extends down to the toes—until the end. And he goes even further. Through a play of echoes between chapters 2 and 3, the text suggests that Nebuchadnezzar not only desires his reign to cover the time span of the statue, but he wants it of an eternal nature,[1] like the kingdom established by God, represented in his dream (chapter 2) by the stone. Significantly, in the Aramaic part of the text, the same word, *haqim* (Dan. 2:44), used to describe the establishment of God's reign (translated "to set up"), becomes in chapter 3 a key word that resounds like a refrain—it appears eight times (verses 1, 2, 3, 5, 7, 12, 14, 18)—to describe the erection of the statue. The kingdom of Nebuchadnezzar replaces God's kingdom.

I. The Babel Complex

This usurpation by the king of Babylon reminds the reader of

44

that by the ancient city of Babel. The common use of the word *biqah* at the head of both passages (Gen. 11:1; cf. Dan. 3:1) already suggests the link between the two. The tower, like the statue, is erected "on the plain," evoking the vast vistas of this region[2]—the space needed for the crowd gathered there to worship together.

Both events most likely occurred in the same place. It is definitely the same geographical area. And if we take the somewhat vague expression of the "plain of Shinar" used in Genesis 11:2 (KJV) in the broader sense as a "province of Babylon," it may well be that it applies to the plain of Dura, also situated "in the province of Babylon" (Dan. 3:1). Archaeological excavations led to the discovery of a spot whose Arabic name still echoes its ancient designation as *Tolul Dura* (mound of Dura). It is located three miles south of ancient Babylon near the River Dura as it joins the Euphrates. The digs even uncovered a platform 19½ feet high with 16½ square yards of surface that could well have served as a support to the statue.[3]

The ceremony to which Nebuchadnezzar calls his guests is, as in the episode of Babel, a religious one. It is a dedication, a *hanukkah* (verses 2, 3). The Bible always uses the word in relation to the altar or the Temple (Num. 7:10; 2 Chron. 7:9). Nebuchadnezzar's intentions are therefore clear: he substitutes the cult of his person for divine adoration. It is therefore not surprising that the whole scenario leads to rituals of adoration. The same gesture of prostration, *sgd,* through which the Nebuchadnezzar of chapter 2 expressed his adoration for God (verse 46), the king now requires of others for his statue. Nebuchadnezzar has replaced God. Such a usurpation of God perfectly reflects the proud tradition of Babel: a movement from below that soars up to claim divine glory and prerogatives.

The parallel between the two events is striking. At the time of Babel "the whole world" clustered in the plain to unite in a common sacred act (Gen. 11:1). Nebuchadnezzar gathers in the same plain not only his officials but all "peoples, nations and men of every language" (Dan. 3:4) to unite them in a sacred ceremony in his honor. Here we discern a fundamental trait of the religion of Babel: it does not tolerate diversity. It is the same passion for unity that we witness among the builders of Babel: "Let us build ourselves *a* city, with *a* tower . . . , so that we may make *a* name for ourselves" (Gen. 11:4).

Both the metals and the measurements of the statue evoke a preoccupation with unity. The statue is entirely of gold. In reaction to the statue in the dream, which consisted of several metals, each representing another kingdom, Nebuchadnezzar casts his statue in one metal only, depicting his own kingdom, the gold. He not only rejects the idea of succession, but also the concept of difference: all is cast in the same mold.

The statue measures 60 cubits high. We must understand the number 60 here in its cultural context. The Sumero-Akkadian numerological system is sexagesimal, unlike the Egyptian system that we have adopted. Interestingly, the sexagesimal system has survived in our conception of time and space: 60 minutes, 60 seconds, 360 degrees, etc. The utilization of a six-cubit measuring stick (approximately 3 meters or 3.3 yards) by the prophet Ezekiel (Eze. 40:5) indicates a Babylonian influence. The measurement of 60 cubits confirms the account's historical authenticity. Moreover, the disproportion between the 60 cubits in length versus only six cubits of width suggests a form resembling more an obelisk than a statue, similar to the many monuments of antiquity that Pliny the Elder would compare to towers.[4] The extreme height echoes the arrogance of a king who seeks to impress the newcomer. But the number 60 points to yet another preoccupation: in Babylonian numerical symbolism 60 represents the notion of unity. In erecting his statue to a height of 60 cubits, Nebuchadnezzar seeks primarily to enforce his will for unity—for one kingdom, one religion. We can better understand his obsession for unity in the light of a recent archaeological finding of a cuneiform tablet dating from the ninth year of his reign (595-594).[5] The tablet relates a certain insurrection that threatened the kingdom's unity.

In the light of such later events, we understand that the king felt compelled to erect his statue as a symbol of unity,[6] as a test to ensure his subordinates' fidelity. Down to our times we know what forms of intolerance such politics have engendered. From Louis XIV to the ayatollahs, not forgetting Hitler and Stalin, it is a historical constant: when unity is the ideal, suspicion falls on any kind of difference. It must then be eliminated. Woe to anyone who cannot squeeze into the mold! Violence becomes the corollary to intolerance. Hence the threat accompanying the call to adoration: "Whoever does not fall down and worship will immediately be thrown into a blazing furnace" (Dan. 3:6).

The religion described in these lines is not the result of a reflection, of a choice, nor the expression of a faith or of a deep experience. Here, we worship because something forces us to do so. We kneel, but the heart is elsewhere. It is a religion of bureaucrats, of sheep, a religion of automatons. And indeed, they are the prototypes we encounter in the plain of Dura.

The passage first cites the bureaucrats, the officials ranking from highest to lowest. We find them all present, recorded by the lengthy list of Daniel in hierarchical order (verse 3). Their adoration is a formality—they are there only because of their position. It is in their best interest to show some zeal, for their religion is their position and success in the social pyramid.

Following the officials comes the crowd. They are like sheep sharing the same feeble, stereotyped bleat. Unable to adore on their own, they need directions, a starting signal, as in a typical totalitarian society. All is in order, in a straight line, as narrated by the text: "They stood before it" (verse 3), ready to raise their hands, or fists, like puppets, as suggested particularly by the repetitious reading of the list of officials when convoked by the king and as they execute his command, and by the refrain of the musical instruments. Nebuchadnezzar then summoned the satraps, prefects, governors, advisers, treasurers, judges, magistrates, and all the other provincial officials to assemble[7] for the dedication of the image he had set up (verse 2).

"So the satraps, prefects, governors, advisers, treasurers, judges, magistrates and all the other provincial officials assembled for the dedication of the image that King Nebuchadnezzar had set up, and they stood before it" (verse 3).

"As soon as you hear the sound of the horn, flute, zither, lyre, harp, pipes and all kinds of music, you must fall down and worship the image of gold that King Nebuchadnezzar has set up" (verse 5).

"Therefore, as soon as they heard the sound of the horn, flute, zither, lyre, harp and all kinds of music, all the peoples, nations and men of every language fell down and worshiped the image of gold that King Nebuchadnezzar had set up" (verse 7).

Lengthy paragraphs, but intentionally so, they highlight the automatic character of such adoration through the satirical technique of repetition. The role played here by music has a significant role, as the narrator mentions numerous instruments of "all kinds," balancing three wind instruments with three string instruments, thus framing the ceremony with the threefold symbol of perfection. Everything is measured, in place. Although it may lack depth, the form is at least maintained. A focus on external organization often seeks to compensate for internal sterility. The administrators are preoccupied with structures and policies as though hinting at an extinction of reflection and faith. The formalism of the religion of Babel prevails over spiritual truth. The primary role of music in such a context is to produce the illusion of religious sentiment.

The ancients knew how to use music to elicit a mystical experience. And indeed, music has long been associated with the use of drugs and the practice of mutilation to induce ecstasy, or *unio mystica*. Everything remains on the level of the emotions and the nervous system. Even today, thanks to the media, we can witness the effect of music on the masses. Singers and musicians exercise tremendous power over crowds of adoring fans. We no longer need lyrics or a coherent message to convince others. The phenomenon has even invaded religious communities. In reaction to the cerebral frigidity of traditional services, certain denominations have fallen into the other extreme. They spoon-feed and wash down the message by the continuous purring of background music. Believers, transported by the spirit, shout and cry out in delirious enthusiasm. Such an approach considers reflection unnecessary and outdated. It only smiles at absolute judgments. This episode in the book of Daniel warns us against a strictly emotional religion. Emotion can be a part of the religious experience only when united with reflection and thought. Adoration must involve the whole being, and to neglect one aspect could lead to bowing before an idol. Likewise, in the plain of Dura, the preachers of Babel do not waste time in dry demonstrations or arguments. Music suffices to trigger adoration, and its adherents live strictly in the present. Several times the passage explicitly stresses the dimension of the present.

"As soon as you hear . . . , you must fall down and worship" (verse 5). Grasped by the emotion conveyed by the music and carried away by the influence of the crowd, each person falls to his or her knees without a thought of tomorrow. It is almost an automatic reflex. The blazing furnace stands nearby as an immediate threat—a custom, by the way, then current in the Middle East. It has been attested at Larsa, south of Babylon, since the seventh century before the Common Era and is a penalty initiated by the Code of Hammurabi (numbers 25 and 110). According to Jewish tradition, Abraham had faced this type of death when he refused to bow to Nimrod's idols.[8] A few years before Daniel, Nebuchadnezzar had roasted two false prophets, Zedekiah and Ahab. Jeremiah referred to death by fire as a curse (Jer. 29:21, 22). In fact, such furnaces were a normal part of the region's landscape, being used in the firing of bricks. Archaeological excavations have revealed several such furnaces in the area surrounding Babylon. Scripture also associates the furnace with the construction of the tower of Babel (Gen. 11:3).

It is also probable that the furnace stood right at the feet of the statue. According to Diodorus of Sicily, the Carthaginians had erected a bronze statue of their god directly on top of a furnace dug below the earth, to which it was the custom to throw live infants to their deaths. Indeed, the concept of furnace was not a vague abstraction in the ancient Middle Eastern mind. Fires blazed with deadly devastation in these dry regions. People would instantly regard the furnace as an immediate danger. Here again, we find the dimension of the present alluded to: "Whoever does not fall down and worship will immediately be thrown into a blazing furnace" (Dan. 3:6). Terrified by the proximity of the threat, their thoughts become embedded in the present and their obedience proceeds solely from the instinct of self-preservation.

Violent and intolerant, totalitarian and mechanical, the religion of Babel is also one that focuses on the present. In any case, it works: everyone obeys. Everyone?

II. The False Charges of the Chaldeans

Again, as in chapter 1, the Jews stand out by their startling behavior. The text does not go into the details of their whereabouts or the means of their resistance. Whether they stayed home or stood alone in the plain, we do not know. In any case they did not go unnoticed. The chapter alludes only to the three Jews, even though likely more were involved, as the text mentions "the Jews." If the Chaldeans focus on *those* three, it is probably because of their high position in the Babylonian political hierarchy. Coming from an ancient tradition of leadership, the Chaldeans viewed the Jews' recent promotions as a threat. Behind their religious and administrative zeal lingers a morbid jealousy. The familiar ghost of anti-Judaism already looms on the horizon with its associated mass murders. For anti-Semites are not only jealous of the Jew, whom they see as a threat occupying the position they envy; they speculate on the national danger Jews represent. Such pseudo-religious piety does not really arise from any sense of adoration, but from personal ambition and nationalistic feelings. We can detect this in the arguments centered on the king rather than on the god: "But there are some Jews . . . who pay no attention to you. . . . They neither serve *your* gods nor worship the image of gold *you* have set up" (verse 12). The accusers are more concerned with the downfall of the Jews than with the adoration of the statue.

The Aramaic expression used to express their accusation is very suggestive. It literally says: "To eat the morsels of the Jews" (verse 8). False charges are a kind of cannibalism. Slandering coworkers is nothing less than threatening their life-sustaining positions. It is an act of devouring. The psychology of the tattletale harbors a latent desire for the rival's death.

As for Daniel, his function as governor or "satrap" put him above the Chaldeans and at the same time out of their reach. His high position exempted him from having to take the oath of loyalty. Furthermore, the possibility remains of his being elsewhere because of his responsibilities. The last words of chapter 2 situate Daniel "at the royal court" (verse 49). Beyond its allusion to Daniel's high position (on the phrase "at the gate," see Ruth 4:1-12; Esther 3:2),

Jewish tradition has interpreted the phrase to imply that Daniel was indeed away at the moment of the dedication of the statue. Thus the Talmud has an idiomatic usage of the phrase to designate a slave who is far away from his master (*Erubin* 72a). In any case, whether geographically or in terms of his official position, Daniel is at least for the moment beyond the grasp of the Chaldeans. The Chaldeans furthermore preferred to ignore the other Jews so as to intimidate the king by numbers. The wisest tactic would be to present a reasonable complaint, thus limiting their victims to the three Jews in question. Moreover, the three Jews were direct threats to their positions, and consequently, the focus of their schemes.

III. In the Fire

But the king hesitates and does not order their immediate execution. He knows them well. For some years now they have been in his service. Instead, he gives them a chance to explain themselves. Nebuchadnezzar inquires whether they had really ignored the royal decree (Dan. 3:14). Perhaps the orders got distorted somewhere along the way. Maybe they did not grasp the seriousness of the situation. The king therefore repeats word-for-word the order to submit in adoration (verse 15). The confrontation that then follows opposes two irreconcilable religious mentalities.

The religion of Nebuchadnezzar, like that of the Chaldeans, is one of the immediate: "Now *when* you hear . . . if you are ready to fall down and worship. . . . But if you do not worship it, you will be thrown *immediately* into a blazing furnace" (verse 15). For him, only the present matters and he does not even consider the future. "What god will be able to rescue you from my hand?" (verse 15). On the other hand, the religion of the Jews essentially centers on the future. "The God we serve is able to save us from it, and he will rescue us from your hand, O king" (verse 17). The Jews go even further. To the "if" (verse 15) of the king that introduces the immediate threat, the Jews echo with the "if" of verse 18 that raises the risk of faith and moves further beyond the bounds of the near future. Both cases employ the same Aramaic expression, *hen la* (if . . . not, otherwise). The contrast between these two conceptions of religion is striking. The "if" of the king points to a mechanical religion of causality: "If you do not worship . . . , you will be thrown" (verse 15), whereas the "if" of the Jews testifies to the grace and liberty upheld by their religion: "If he does not [deliver] . . . know, O king, that we will not serve your gods" (verse 18). Such behavior goes beyond the king's comprehension. It dawns on him that the Jews situate themselves outside his will. Looking beyond the immediate, they maintain hope in a future. In the face of failure, they answer by unconditional service.

Here lies the difference between idolatry and the religion of Israel. Idolatry is a religion fashioned in humanity's image. The worshiper manipulates the idol-object to bless or curse automatically. The religion of Israel, however, is a revelation from above, of a living God with whom we can establish a personal relationship that not only implies an exchange of love but also of questions. That is why, even when this God does not save, even if He does not bless, the Jew can remain faithful *in spite of* . . .

Nebuchadnezzar gives them opportunity to defend themselves as he argues and threatens, but to no avail. The Jews, the text tells us, refuse to answer (verse 16). The Aramaic term "to answer" also means "to defend oneself." The Jews oppose the king in a nonviolent way that leaves him in a state of confusion and helplessness. To the religion of Babel centered on the present and consequently legalistic, formalist, and violent, the Jews champion a religion focused on the future and consequently free, unconditional, and nonviolent.

Pushed beyond his limits, the king loses control. The text tells us that "his attitude toward them changed" (verse 19). The Aramaic literally states that his "countenance changed." The king reacts with anger and violence in response to the serene assurance of the Jews. He orders that his servants heat the furnace "seven times hotter" (verse 19), that is, to its maximum (see Prov. 24:16; 26:16), as though the previous temperature had been insufficient. Guards throw the Jews in with all their clothes on. The victims have no time to prepare psychologically.

Costing the lives of the executioners as it does, the reaction shows how disturbed and anguished the king is. It is as though he anticipates the coming miracle. He is, in fact, the first one to notice the inconceivable, the first to react. Barely has the passage mentioned that the three men have been "bound" and "thrown" into the furnace (Dan. 3:21) than the king sees "four men walking around in the fire, unbound and unharmed" (verse 25). Not only are the three Jews untouched and free but, as pointed out not without humor by the text, they are "walking around" (verse 25), testifying of a God who mocks human power.

But who is the mysterious fourth person? Nebuchadnezzar is more or less conscious of the link between that fourth person and the miracle. Intrigued, he gazes upon a being resembling a "son of the gods" (verse 25). In Semitic languages, the term "son of" renders in an idiomatic way the nature of what is qualified. In this way, a "son of twenty years" means 20 years old (Ex. 30:14); "son of man" means belonging to human nature (Jer. 49:18); "son of cattle" means having a bovine nature (Num. 15:8); "son of death" means of mortal nature (1 Sam. 2:31), etc. The king concludes that the fourth being has a divine nature. Significantly, the Septuagint translates it as "angel of God," a designation used again in verse 28. In the Hebrew Bible the "angel of God" functions as God's representative and is sometimes identified with God Himself (see Gen. 16:10-13; 21:17; 22:15, 16; Hosea 12:4; Gen. 32:28, etc.). Scripture gives such beings the title, according to Metzudos, "because we view them as if they were part of the Divine household."[9] When he spots the fourth figure in the fire, Nebuchadnezzar has no more doubts as to the miracle's origin. He calls out to the three Jews, inviting them to step out, admitting thereby his defeat. Humiliated, the king understands he now faces a God totally out of the ordinary. He cannot but remember his dream, and recognizes that he is dealing with that same God. The expression by which he designates Him as "the Most High" (Dan. 3:26) alludes to his chapter 2 confession of the "God of gods" (Dan. 2:47).

Here again the miracle is not a result of human power and technology but solely God's doing. We are now outside the world of magicians. A fourth person was needed for the miracle to occur. That salvation comes from without, not from within, is the first lesson we can derive from the divine presence manifested in the fourth person. No matter how righteous and just one is, salvation remains the business of a God who does not lock Himself in heaven or in an attitude of indifference. Because God loves, He chooses to come down to the human level. To save others from the fire, the God of love must Himself pass through it. Because He Himself wants our companionship, He walks with us (Dan. 3:25). But His action does not limit itself to companionship. God also saves. The three Jews step out of the burning furnace (verse 26).

Immediately the crowd gathers around them, wanting to touch, to be sure they are allright. "They saw that the fire had not harmed their bodies, nor was a hair of their heads singed; their robes were not scorched, and there was no smell of fire on them" (verse 27). From head to toes, they remain unscathed. The God of the Jews did not just stop by to comfort them, nor to assure them of His sympathy, but also saved them from the fire.

The God of the Bible is primarily the deity who saves. He is not just the God of a mystical, sentimental, or even intellectual experience. Religion is more than an impression—it situates itself beyond opinions. The satraps and all the king's officials now understand that the God of the Jews is not only the God who comes down, but also the God who has power over death. The Babylonians look upon the three Jews as resurrected beings. After all, they have survived death. By this miracle God defines Himself as being the Creator: "But now, this is what the Lord says—he who created you, O Jacob, he who formed you, O Israel: . . . When you walk through the fire, you will not be burned; the flames will not set you ablaze" (Isa. 43:1, 2).

Only the Creator can save from fire; only He can transform death into life. The three Jews are themselves stunned, unable to utter a word. But their silence also echoes to their last words spoken before the king: "We do not need to defend ourselves before you in this matter" (Dan. 3:16). The answer lies in the event. Words are superfluous in the face of evidence. The very fact that they stand alive and well testifies of their faith in God. We would have expected a long speech commenting and elaborating on the matter, but the three Jews remain silent.

Here is powerful lesson for those always eager to testify, to preach, to boast of God's action in their lives! The behavior of the

Jews reminds us that the silent witness often speaks louder than even the most moving testimonies. Authentic experience has no use for words. Where salvation and truth are concerned, when we deal with what is essential too many words can be suspect. Their noise and multiplicity often camouflage our own hollowness and uncertainty, as though we are seeking to convince ourselves of a truth not yet fully grasped. It is the absence of depth that generates the smooth talker. We concoct well-turned phrases that we then unleash when occasion allows, but in essence, we really have nothing to say.

IV. The Revenge

The Jews remain silent while the others speak for them. But that makes their testimony all the more convincing.

The king now meets the Chaldeans' false charges against the Jews head-on. The command *(teem)* of the king (verse 10) to adore the golden image now becomes the command *(teem)* prohibiting any misrepresentation of the Jews' God (verse 29).

Here again, the king prefers to avoid direct contact with the Hebrew Deity. Although he has come face-to-face with Him, Nebuchadnezzar acts and speaks as though nothing happened. He saw the four men, and his attention focused in the fourth (verse 25), yet he beckons only three of them to join him and ignores the other. He admittedly introduces his discourse with the traditional "Praise be to God" (verse 28),[10] but remains intrinsically detached from the God of heaven—he is only making an objective observation.

His theology is correct. Nebuchadnezzar defined this God as a being who saves and as a unique deity. But for him, this God exists and acts only in relation to the Jews. It is not his deity. Nor is He in the absolute sense. We can sense Nebuchadnezzar's ambiguity and distance in his words: "The God *of* Shadrach, Meshach Abednego," who "rescued *his* servants!" because "they trusted in *him* . . . and were willing to give up their lives rather than serve or worship any god except *their own* God" (verse 28). For him, the religion of Israel remains a tribal affair. He interprets the attitude of the Jews as the courageous and heroic response of a people who stick to their own ethics. He does not consider it as an act of faith in the universal God,

55

the only true God. Nebuchadnezzar admits only that the power of the Hebrew God obviously surpasses that of the other deities: "For no other god can save in this way" (verse 29). But that in no way implies a personal relationship on his part. It is out of the question for him to convert to another religion. One can for an instant be amazed and even disturbed by the strength of the argument, or recognize the uniqueness and superiority of a truth, and still fall back on the more convenient position of "to each his own religion." It is wiser, then, for one to stay where one belongs and avoid the unnecessary confrontations, the uprooting, and even the uncertainties of religious exploration and growth. After all, it requires a lot of courage to apply the lessons of truth to actual concrete existence. We all know to what degree our little habits of thought or of action, of food or of drink, are harmful but that does not imply that we are ready to change them. Such is human nature. It is easier to continue to err, even if we know it, than to break away and walk according to truth. The more integrated one is in a society, the harder this is to do. For the kings, the priests, those who possess political power, for the rich, for those who have succeeded—for all those who are comfortable in a system and respectable, such an undertaking is almost inconceivable.

At least the king authorizes a decree legalizing the Jews' religion. From now on, on pain of death no one can slander or misrepresent the Hebrew God. The situation is now reversed. The same public summoned to adore the image—"The people of any nation or language" (verse 29)—must now respect the religion of others.

Such a decree has little to do with tolerance. Nor is it a question of respecting the other religions. In fact, the only religion mentioned is that of the Jews. What of the others? Given all the conquests by the Babylonian army, we know that the most diverse religions cohabited under Babylonian sovereignty. The throng represents "all the peoples." Yet the religion of Israel is the only one worthy of recognition, given the recent events. In the king's mind Israelite religion is superior to that of the others, and therefore alone worth mentioning. The decree does not show the king's tolerance of other religions, but testifies to the discovery of a truth that disturbs him—

disturbs him to the point that he feels compelled to support his decree with a threat. In fact, any "missionary" zeal that points a raging finger and calls upon the "wrath of God" seeks only to divert attention from one's responsibilities. It is wrong ever to consider religious violence as an expression of a profound conviction. Murder and war, the tortures of the Inquisition, and all the repressive measures taken in the name of religion are symptomatic of spiritual cowardice and anguish. To compensate for religious failure, fanatics themselves become God and assume the right to kill. It is the crime of Cain, the first occurrence of religious intolerance, that would introduce unending brutality into human history. Cain kills Abel not because of a conviction of his own truth or because Abel is wrong, but because of his religious failure, because he is unable to answer to God.[11]

V. The Success of the Jews

Nebuchadnezzar does not convert to the religion of the three Jews. Instead, he legalizes it and personally handles the promotion of its three representatives. In fact, his actions do not really hide the awkwardness of his situation and actually betray something else (see chapter 2). By assuring the success of the three Jews, Nebuchadnezzar seeks to keep a good conscience before this God whom he really wishes to avoid.

For the Chaldeans and the Jews, this conclusion carries yet another lesson. First of all, the use in the concluding verse of the same expression ("in the province of Babylon") as in the opening verse suggests a return to the initial state of affairs. The plotting of the Chaldeans was to no avail. The three Jews are back in their midst and have not even been transferred. They savor their success "in the presence of [their] enemies" (Ps. 23:5). At the end of the ordeal the situation of the Jews has improved, just as in the preceding chapters. Previously, the Jews *were* in the province of Babylon, now they *prosper* in the province of Babylon. Before, there was only one of them—now there are four. The Jews come out of the ordeal enriched. In taking the risk of losing it all, they have gained beyond their expectations. But the Jews had never sought success. They even gave up whatever success, position, or life they had. Their sole preoccupation was to serve and adore God. The kingdom of God belongs to those who do not seek their own interests. It is not a reward for the righteous who through good works come to deserve it. The "success" of the Jews teaches us that the grace of God is never expected, but is reserved for those who have lost everything and who expect nothing in return.

STRUCTURE OF DANIEL 3

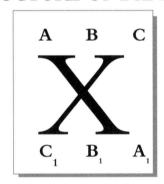

A (verses 1-7)
> The king set up an image in the province of Babylon.
> > **B (verses 2-12)**
> > > An accusation against the Jews
> > > **A** decree against the Jews
> > > **C (verses 13-23)**
> > > > The Jews cast into the furnace
> > > > Dialogue: the king and the Jews
> > > **C_1 (verses 24-27)**
> > > > The Jews saved from the furnace
> > > > Dialogue: the king and the Jews
> > **B_1 (verses 28, 29)**
> > > A blessing on behalf of the Jews
> > > A decree on behalf of the Jews
> **A_1 (verse 30)**
> > The Jews are promoted in the province of Babylon.

---

[1] Regarding this context, it is interesting to note an inscription of Nebuchadnezzar (Wadi-Brisa) in which the king refers to a statue he erected in Lebanon, also symbolizing the eternity of his kingdom: "Beside my statue as king . . . I wrote an inscription mentioning my name, . . . I erected for posterity. . . . May my offspring rule forever" (James B. Pritchard, ed., *Ancient Near Eastern Texts Relating to the Old Testament,* 2nd ed. [Princeton: 1955], p. 307). Obviously it is not the same statue as the one in our text, but the inscription testifies to the king's affinity with statues and corroborates in this way the biblical narrative.

[2] See André Parrot, *The Tower of Babel* (New York: 1955), p. 15.

[3] Oppert, *Expédition Scientifique en Mésopotamie,* vol. 1, pp. 238ff.

[4] Pliny *Natural History* 34. 18.

[5] See William H. Shea, "Daniel 3: Extra-Biblical Texts and the Convocation on the Plain of Dura," *Andrews University Seminary Studies* 20, No. 1 (1982): 29-52.

[6] Such a concern for political unity would explain the trip of Zedekiah to Babylon in the fourth year of his reign, around 594 B.C.E. (see Jer. 51:59-64).

[7] The passage uses the same word *knsh* in the convocation (verse 2) as well as in the execution (verse 3); we render this by the word "assemble."

[8] Babylonian Talmud *Pesaḥim* 118a; see also Moses Alshekh in his commentary on Daniel (*habezelet hasharon, The Rose of Sharon* [Venice: 1592]).

[9] Scherman and Zlotowitz, p. 128.

[10] Cf. Gen. 14:20; 1 Kings 1:48; 1 Chron. 16:36; Ezra 7:27; Ps. 18:46; 28:6; 31:22; 66:20; etc.

[11] See Jacques Doukhan, "A propos du crime de Cain," *Conscience et Liberté* (1976), note 12, pp. 44-48.

CHAPTER 4

THE TREE IN THE MIDDLE OF THE EARTH

For the first time the book of Daniel presents a smiling Nebuchadnezzar. Up to now, his expression had always been one of anger. In chapter 1 Nebuchadnezzar attacks and besieges Jerusalem (verse 1). The king threatens to cut people "into pieces" and to turn houses "into piles of rubble" in chapter 2 (verse 5). Then in chapter 3 he orders everyone to bow and worship, threatening them with a "blazing furnace" (verses 1-6). That same king, once the terror of his own people, now greets them by a generous *shalom:* "Peace be multiplied to you" (Dan. 4:1, NKJV).

For the first time he evokes "the Most High God" (verse 2). Until then Nebuchadnezzar had referred to Him only indirectly through the person of Daniel. Now for the first time he recognizes the God of the Hebrews in an absolute sense, as a deity superior to the other gods, and even as a personal God: "miraculous signs and wonders that the *Most High* God has performed for *me.*"

In the preceding chapters Nebuchadnezzar appeared only to give orders. Now, for the first time, his words do not lash out in command. Instead, they represent a spontaneous testimony to what God has done for him. For once, the king is in a good mood: "It is my pleasure . . ." Nebuchadnezzar does not speak because he must, but because he likes to. The cruel, vindictive ruler whom we had grown to fear has become a poet, breaking into song about the Most High.

I. Signs and Wonders

His heart still full of the miracles he has experienced, Nebuchadnezzar lets his soul overflow with praises. *It is the third prayer of the book of Daniel.* Although composed by a pagan king, the prayer is nevertheless exemplary and beautiful. Reading the passage, the Talmudic rabbis exclaimed: "The king has stolen all the songs and praises from David."[1]

His first words are a cry, an exclamation repeated in a three-word rhythm:

"Signs, how grandiose!

Wonders, how mighty!" (literal translation of first part of verse 3).

The syntax of the Aramaic phrase emphasizes each first word ("signs," "wonders") so as better to render the king's admiration.

By definition, the function of signs and wonders is to attract attention by their extraordinary character, thus evoking another reality invisible to human perception.

Seeing such wonders, the king intuitively senses that reality. Nebuchadnezzar does not merely marvel at the miracles—he also perceives, through the miracle of the present, the miracle of the future, the kingdom of God. For him, the miracle is not only a sign of his being blessed and successful on earth, but also a pointer to another world, of a kingdom to come.

The poem here develops in a double parallelism in a three-word rhythm:

"His kingdom (is) an eternal kingdom

His dominion from generation to generation" (verse 3, literal translation).

This truth is probably the most difficult for Nebuchadnezzar to accept. Ever since his dream of the statue the Babylonian ruler could never admit that his kingdom was only the head. As son of the god Marduk, he wanted his kingdom to be eternal. For the first time, he understands that eternity is a characteristic of God's kingdom alone. It is the only lasting kingdom. Although king of Babylon, Nebuchadnezzar recognizes for the first time the existence of an authority over him. And he goes even further when he acknowledges that God's dominion extends from "generation to generation." Not only the present generation, but all upcoming ones submit to His authority.

But the miracle was but a foretaste of things to come. Nebuchadnezzar now longs for more, for another kind of joy, for another kingdom. The miracle has brought with it no lasting solution. Sickness and obstacles will again pop up at the next turning point. The raison d'être for the miracle is essentially to produce, in a flash of consciousness, the recognition of that other world.

The prayer of Nebuchadnezzar longs for the kingdom to come. Springing from the miracle, it, like all true prayers, testifies to the kingdom of God.

A dream has made him for the first time understand how ephemeral everything is. The horrible dream overwhelmed him at a time when he was most at ease, plunging him to the depths of his existence and being.

II. The Exposition of the Dream

"I, Nebuchadnezzar, was at home in my palace, contented and prosperous. I had a dream . . ." His serenity is from the beginning suspect. The Aramaic word used to denote his peace (verse 4) already hints at the dream that will shake him up. The adjective *raanan* most often characterizes a tree at its prime (Deut. 12:2; Isa. 57:5). The dream compares Nebuchadnezzar to a blossoming tree. At first sight, nothing in the tree suggests an upcoming tragedy, and yet tragedy hits. The dream is quite bizarre, and no one dares interpret it. He consults all kinds of sages: The *hartumayya*, Egyptian magicians expert in the interpretation of dreams (Gen. 41:8). The *ashpayya*, Akkadian priests and exorcists. The Chaldean astrologers, well versed in the art of prediction. The *gazarayya*, interpreters of the gods' decrees *(gazar)*. All are doomed to fail (Dan. 4:7). As last resort (verse 8), Daniel speaks. One may wonder why Nebuchadnezzar didn't summon him immediately, aware as he was that the "spirit of the holy gods" was in the Hebrew prophet and that "no mystery" was "too difficult" for him (verse 9). According to the text, it seems that the king even ignored Daniel for a long time. All the wise men received a summons to appear before the king except Daniel, who came at his own initiative. Cornered, Nebuchadnezzar now had no choice but to hear the Hebrew prophet's interpretation. As in chapter 2, the king refuses to face a reality that does not fit his own aspirations. Once again, an unexpected truth hits him, a disturbing truth like any of divine origin.

But even then Nebuchadnezzar shies away from it. His main concern now is to keep up appearances. He recognizes Daniel's superiority ("the spirit of the holy gods is in him") but manages to slip in the phrase "He is called Belteshazzar, after the name of my god" (verse 8). The king attributes Daniel's power to his Babylonian god. His humility just masks his pride.

When seen against the background of his pride and unconscious happiness, Nebuchadnezzar's dream takes on a whole different meaning. Its narration and interpretation develop in two stages, both introduced by a parallel reference to what the king saw (verses 10, 13, 20, 23). The first stage is positive and involves a tree at its prime. The second is negative, and tells of the tree's fate.

III. The Explanation of the Dream
1. The Tree at Its Prime

The tree symbolism was not strange to Nebuchadnezzar. Herodotus tells of the case of Astyages, Nebuchadnezzar's brother-in-law, who had also dreamed of a tree symbolizing his dominion over part of the world.[2] Nebuchadnezzar himself, in an inscription, compares Babylon to a great tree sheltering the nations of the world.[3] Moreover, the parallel between the tree and the statue of chapter 2 is sufficiently clear for Nebuchadnezzar to understand some of the dream's basic message. The passage describes the protection provided by the tree in the same terms as in chapter 2. Daniel says of Nebuchadnezzar in chapter 2: "In your hands he has placed mankind and the beasts of the field and the birds of the air" (verse 38). Chapter 4 declares of the tree: "Under it the beasts of the field found shelter, and the birds of the air lived in its branches; from it every creature was fed" (verse 12). Like the head of the statue, the tree is visible from "the ends of the earth" (verse 11).

The narrator identifies the tree with the head of the statue, and it represents Nebuchadnezzar.

The metaphor of the tree alludes also to the king's presumptuous character, comparing Nebuchadnezzar to Adam in his function as manager of the universe (Gen. 1:28). It also hints at the tree of life (or the tree of the knowledge of good and evil) in its position in the middle of the earth (Gen. 2:9; 3:3). The tree stretches unto the heavens (Dan. 4:11, 20). Clearly it is no ordinary tree. Everything points to its superiority.

But underneath all this foliage of praise is a layer of harsh criticism. For it is the pride of Nebuchadnezzar that the image of the tree in fact depicts. Ezekiel uses the same metaphor to represent Assyria's pride (Eze. 31:3-9). The Ezekiel passage shares many common motifs with Daniel 4. There also the tree shelters the birds and the beasts (verse 6). In addition, the tree is planted in the middle of the garden (verse 9) and surpasses all the others in height (verses 2, 5). The text of Daniel is but an echo of the passage in Ezekiel. The pride of the king is proportional to the height of the tree: "Because it towered on high, lifting its top above the thick foliage, and because it was proud of its height" (verse 10).

This tree which stretches up to the heavens, sheltering and majestic, is in fact an open insult to God. (Interestingly, the New Testament employs the same tree imagery to represent God's kingdom [Luke 13:19].) The dream tree symbolizes the pride of a king who intends to replace God. But Nebuchadnezzar has no question as to what the tree depicts. In the light of his own Babylonian culture and most of all of his first dream, he cannot but recognize that the tree stands for himself. And with this in mind, no wonder the Babylonian king prefers to rely on the astrologers' explanation. Therefore, when Daniel enters the scene, he trembles and his first words are full of tact and wishing: "My lord, if only the dream applied to your enemies . . . !" (Dan. 4:19). But the interpretation that follows slashes like a knife: "You, O king, are that tree!" (verse 22).

2. The Fall of the Tree

A crashing descent from above (verse 23), like the ancient story of Babel (Gen. 11:4, 5) suddenly halts the growth of the tree. The first scene of the dream was visual and static in its depiction of a magnificent tree. The second scene has sound and is dynamic as the king views the movements of celestial beings and hears their commanding voices. The first scene, peaceful and majestic, contrasts the second scene, tumultuous and disturbing. From the serenity of the initial description we now move to violent activity.

The identity of these celestial beings already suggests a change in the king's destiny: "One of those who keep watch" (literal translation Dan. 4:13, 17, 23). It is the only occurrence in the Bible of such a being. The dream here speaks the language of the king. According to an ancient Babylonian belief, as attested in the Zoroastrian commentary of the Zend-Avesta, the great god had placed four celestial watchmen over the four corners of the heavens and over the astral movements.[4]

Nebuchadnezzar understands the presence of the celestial beings as meaning that the great God of heaven is determining his destiny. The dream, however, portrays the beings according to biblical tradition, presenting them as "holy ones," a term usually applied to angels in many biblical texts (Job 5:1; 15:15; Ps. 89:7, 8; Zech. 14:5). The Septuagint follows this line of interpretation in its translation of the word "watchman" by the word "angel." The "watchman," or angel of heaven, announces the destiny of the king in two sentences.

The first sentence consists of several commands concerning the tree (Dan. 4:14, 23). Once cut down, the tree disappears from sight. Stripped of its branches, leaves, and fruit, it loses its universal nurturing and sheltering function (verses 14, 21). The oracle means that the king would be "driven away from people" (verse 25).

The second sentence contains only one command concerning the state of the tree after its destruction (verse 15). The tree, fallen and stripped, is anchored to the ground so as to stop further growth. The use of iron and bronze chains, known for their strength (2 Chron. 24:12), guarantees that the tree will not grow as long as they are there. The verb used suggests a tree "imprisoned" *(asar)* in an animal state. The language of the dream identifies the stump of the tree with a beast. In fact, it does have a beastly appearance. It resides among the "wild animals" (Dan. 4:25), sleeps with them, is "drenched with the dew of heaven" (verses 15, 23), eats "grass like cattle" (verse 25), and even thinks like them: "Let his mind be changed from that of a man and let him be given the mind of an animal" (verse 16).

The substitution of an animal mind for a human one is, for Daniel, the key to this strange metamorphosis. Nebuchadnezzar will cease to be a beast only when he recognizes that "the Most High is sovereign over the kingdoms of men" (verse 25). In other words, the animal state of the king is linked to his religious unawareness. The king has no real knowledge of God.

From a biblical point of view, the king could not stoop any lower. Confined to an animal state, he cannot be delivered. He hears the oracle as a "decree" from above (verse 24) and it is definitive and absolute. God has even fixed the time involved: "seven times" (verse 25). The number is sacred, pointing to the decree's divine origin.

But the oracle still leaves room for hope. After all, the actual fall of the tree has not yet taken place in the dream. Nebuchadnezzar only hears orders about it. The moment to execute the prophecy has not yet arrived. Indeed, Nebuchadnezzar stands tall, at his prime. He still has time to reverse the oracle. "Renounce your sins by doing what is right, and your wickedness by being kind to the oppressed. It may be that then your prosperity will continue" (verse 27). Twice Daniel reminds the king that recognizing God will save him (verse 26). The solution is a religious one and concerns his relationship with the God of heaven. But it also has an ethical aspect that involves his fellow humans. The prophet exhorts Nebuchadnezzar to be just and compassionate (verse 27). Repentance involves a horizontal as well as a vertical dimension. Only by recognizing a God that transcends him will Nebuchadnezzar be able to respect the poor and practice justice (tsedaqa). It is the awareness of Someone outside of self that forms the basis of respect for others. The fear of God, that is, our consciousness that God is watching us, prevents debauchery and obliges one to justice. On the other hand, it is unthinkable to cherish a relationship with God when one is on bad terms with others. The love of God implies the love of the neighbor. To murder another person is to murder the image of God (Gen. 9:6). Likewise, to ignore God is to despise others. Ethics and religion are inter-twined, one implying the other. According to Daniel, the king's re-pentance is still possible; he still has a window of escape (Dan. 4:27).

The outcome of the decree is then the king's responsibility. His destiny rests in his own hands. Nebuchadnezzar is free. But there re-mains still a note of uncertainty. The oracle introduces the assurance of prosperity, in the case of repentance, with the conjunction *hen,* meaning "maybe." Even if the king repents, God's benediction can-not be certain. God too is free to act as He wills. Nebuchadnezzar should not repent in order to gain his prosperity back, but because he understands the gravity of his sin. Otherwise, his response would not be sincere or of free choice. With his own interest in mind, Nebuchadnezzar would not repent because he wanted to, but be-cause he had to, in order to preserve his well-being. To be free, and therefore authentic, repentance must be unconditional.

Likewise, we cannot force God to bless and reward the just. He would not be a sovereign God then, but a vending machine. God is free, like human beings. We should receive His blessings as a grace, bestowed independently of our good deeds.

A ray of hope now penetrates the gloom of the dream: anything is possible. And even if repentance does not result in forgiveness, even if the oracle comes to pass and the tree collapses before the blow of the ax, even then there remains a way out. The life of the tree is not threatened, nor is it uprooted. The trunk and roots *(iqqar)* remain. Although cut down, the tree has the prospect of a new spring. The fixed amount of time (seven times), implying that there will be an end to the ordeal, itself offers hope. Even in the darkest hour, hope lingers on.

IV. The Fulfillment of the Dream
1. The Pride of the King

Daniel tells both the interpretation of the dream as well as its ful-fillment. In both cases, the king cannot speak, first because Daniel is speaking, and in the second case because the king is no longer capa-ble of speech anymore. This second silence is also part of the fulfill-ment of the prophecy. The third person singular of the passage suggests that the king cannot speak for himself anymore. He has become just an object. The prophecy's fulfillment is situated in time and in space, as a historical event. It comes to pass one year later, on the anniversary of the dream, in the royal palace.

The king wallows in his satisfaction over his accomplishments, unaware of what is about to befall him. We find him "walking on the roof of the royal palace" admiring the fruits of his prosperity (verses 29, 30). But this time the text much more explicitly points out the king's underlying pride: "Is not this the great Babylon I have built as the royal residence, by my mighty power and for the glory of my majesty?" (verse 30).

And indeed, Babylon was worthy of praise. Nebuchadnezzar did make his mark in history as the greatest builder of Babylon, unlike his predecessors, who were mainly conquerors. Earlier monarchs preferred to live in the city of their choice and came to Babylon only on special occasions. For Nebuchadnezzar, however, the city was his royal residence, "the city of his pride."[5] And indeed, Babylon owes him her greatest landmarks. Stretching more than three square miles, with its palace, its suspended gardens, and its 50 temples, Babylon had one of the seven marvels of the ancient world and was one of the greatest cities at the time.

According to the testimony of the Babylonian priest Berossus and of ancient cuneiform tablets, Nebuchadnezzar was the principal architect of the city.[6] In addition to the numerous temples and fortified walls, the king built his palace, in his own words "as a monument to the genius and might of the kings of Babylon."[7] The hanging gardens were also his creation, to remind his wife Amytis of the trees, flowers, and hills of her native Media. The city's grandiose beauty made a lasting impression on travelers and poets.

But it was pride that propelled Nebuchadnezzar to undertake this work. And it is through the eyes of pride that he would later contemplate his creation—not only as told in the Bible, but also as related by cuneiform inscriptions. Some 50 tablets authored by Nebuchadnezzar himself witness to his feelings. Nebuchadnezzar writes about the palace: "I built this palace, seat of my kingship over the mighty kings . . . palace of joy, of rejoicing. . . . In Babylon, I ed-

ified it, on top of the ancient trough . . . with mortar and bricks I se-
cured its foundations."[8] Or, about the city of Babylon as a whole: "I
have made Babylon, the holy city, the glory of the great gods, more
prominent than before. . . . No king . . . has ever created, no earlier
king has ever built, what I have magnificently built for Marduk."[9]
Prophecy had predicted the king's pride as it depicts him as a mighty
tree, its branches reaching the heavens, striving for divinity.

Interestingly, the text reminds the reader of the story of Babel.
Like Nebuchadnezzar, the builders of the Tower of Babel wanted it
to "reach to the heavens." Like the Babylonian king, they sought to
"make a name for ourselves" (Gen. 11:4). And likewise, a voice
from heaven interrupts their work (verses 5-7), distorting their language into one incomprehensible bellow (verse 9).

2. The Insane King

The symptoms. The king starts acting like an animal, eating,
sleeping, and thinking like an ox. Paradoxically, in seeking to surpass
other humans, he has fallen below humanity. Anyone ambitious for
success should carefully ponder its meaning. When one has reached
the top, what other alternative is there but to plunge back down?

Nebuchadnezzar's little adventure seems to have other parallels
in ancient history. In the *Babylonian Job* (1600-1150 B.C.E.) we read:
"Like a she-*nâkim* or a *šûkû*-demon he made my finger-nails grow."[10]

The novel of Ahikar (seventh century B.C.E.) has a character
say: "I would stoop to the earth, my hair falling upon my shoulders,
my beard down to my chest, my body was covered with dust, and
my nails were as the eagle's."[11]

Today psychiatrists have diagnosed Nebuchadnezzar's behavior
as a variant of paranoia and schizophrenia.[12] Historian of psychiatry
Gregory Zilboorg relates several such cases between the third and
seventeenth centuries C.E.[13]

As rare and strange as the illness may seem, it has been a constant
throughout history. Today it has practically disappeared in industri-
alized countries, where it is adequately treated, but traces of it appear
in China, India, Africa, and South America. In recent years several
cases have found their way to the hospitals of Paris and Bordeaux.[14]

The symptoms are always the same. The patient imagines that he has been transformed into a wolf (lycanthropy), an ox (boanthropy), or another animal (dog, leopard, snake, crocodile), and behaves as such down to the most intimate details. The illusion of the patient is so perfect that it affects even the way he sees himself. A 49-year-old woman was convinced her head was that of a wolf complete with snout and fangs. And when she opened her mouth to speak, she would hear herself growl and howl like a beast.[15]

If we are to believe the historians and psychiatrists mentioned above, the "Nebuchadnezzar syndrome" seems to have truly existed. Of course, we meet with complete silence as far as Babylonian official chronicles are concerned. Still, a number of extrabiblical sources seem to support the biblical story.

Three centuries after the death of Nebuchadnezzar, the Babylonian priest Berosus tells us that "after forty-three years of reign, Nebuchadnezzar fell ill on the construction site of a wall . . . and died."[16] This link between the illness of the king and construction reminds us of the biblical narrative. Moreover, the special mention of a period of illness preceding death hints at the special character that disease may have had.

A Greek historian Abydenus (third century B.C.E.) testifies that Nebuchadnezzar became "possessed by a god or something of the sort, climbed up to his palace's terrace pronouncing prophetic words, and disappeared suddenly."[17] Again we find several motifs in common with the biblical text: the king's location on the terrace, a prophecy, and his unexplained disappearance.

Finally, the recent discovery of cuneiform tablets confirms the biblical narration. In 1975 the Assyriologist A. K. Grayson published a cuneiform text, now conserved in the British Museum (BM 34113 = sp213), that alludes to Nebuchadnezzar's insanity. It seems that for a while "his life appeared of no value," he gave senseless and contradictory orders, and he could not express affection to either his son or his daughter, recognize his clan, or even participate in the building up of Babylon and of its temple.[18]

Considering history and psychiatric diagnoses, the story of Daniel sounds possible.

The time. According to the biblical text, Nebuchadnezzar remained in his pathological condition for a period of "seven times." To situate the illness in time gives it a certain degree of historicity. The text locates the event right after the king finished his special building projects in Babylon. Several elements suggest that we should translate the Aramaic word *idan* in the sense of "years":

1. Significantly, the illness of the king starts precisely "after twelve months," implying that one should keep on counting in terms of additional 12-month periods. The year is the basic unity into which we should convert prophetic "times."

2. The relationship between these two periods of time (12 months and seven years) is outlined in the style of the text. The two expressions "twelve months" and "seven years" echo each other, since similar Aramaic wording ("at the end of that time," *liqsath* [verses 29 and 34]) introduce both of them.

3. The etymology of the word *idan* (time) is related to the word *od* (to repeat, to return, to redo), hinting at a repetition of the same time, or of the same season (Dan. 2:21) of each new year.

4. Daniel 7:25 defines *idan* as being a year, a concept we find even more explicit in the parallel passage of Revelation 12:14 (see later chapters).

5. The Septuagint and the medieval rabbis (Rashi, Ibn Ezra, etc.) retain the interpretation based on the sense of "years."

When the passage uses the word "times" instead of "years," it is to draw our attention to the number seven, symbol of the divine. And indeed, the illness is not of natural causes, but divinely inflicted. The end of Nebuchadnezzar's trial is "sealed" (Dan. 4:16, 34). God controls his destiny, and nobody can change it.

V. Prayer of the Dead

That is, nobody can alter it but the king himself: "I, Nebuchadnezzar, raised my eyes toward heaven, and my sanity was restored" (verse 34). No matter how severe the case of lycanthropy, the patient always retains a fragment of consciousness and experiences occasional moments of lucidity. Even in the grip of mental illness a person remains human, never entirely losing his or her potential for liberty and free will. Psychiatrists, aware of this, therefore refuse to classify their patients under the irrevocable label of "crazy." Instead, they consider the patient as a sick person, implying that there always exists a potential for improvement.

Our passage reveals even the most rigid determinism can be swayed by human liberty. Even in the pit of bestiality, one can look up and be reunited with humanity. All Nebuchadnezzar had to do was raise his eyes toward heaven (verse 34). Nebuchadnezzar became a beast when he thought of himself as a god and looked down from the roof of his royal palace. But he regained his humanity when he knew himself as a beast and looked up from the dust of his animal abode. The paradox is invaluable, both on a psychological and a theological level.

It is impossible for the human self to develop without first knowing its limitations. Whoever thinks they're a bird will throw themselves through a window and land in very bad shape on the pavement below. To be able to fly, one must cultivate an awareness of the laws of gravity and work around them. Here we find the secret of liberty and happiness. But there is yet another lesson, this time concerning salvation. Only one who is capable of seeing beyond his or her own self can be saved. Salvation is from without, not from within. Like Nebuchadnezzar, we must raise our eyes toward heaven. When the king discovers this truth in the depth of his own soul, his sanity comes back with his faith, confirming biblical tradition: "The fool says in his heart, 'There is no God'" (Ps. 53:1; 14:1). The illusion is to think that it is an illusion to believe. For Daniel, faith and reason are compatible. Faith emerges out of reason and is a fundamental characteristic of reason.

Nebuchadnezzar's experience has universal implications. Beyond the healing of the king, we perceive the miracle of resurrection. Already the first words of this section hint at this: "At the end of days" (literal translation, verse 34). Daniel 12:13 uses the same words in relation to resurrection. The "resurrection" of Nebuchadnezzar paves the way for the resurrection "at the end of days." The Babylonian king wakes up from his stupor and speaks. Up until now the passage has referred to him in the third person. Having regained consciousness, he is again able to speak in the first person. His first words are a prayer—*the fourth prayer of the book of Daniel.*

Still covered with dust, his eyes grasping the heavens, Nebuchadnezzar lets his thoughts alternate between heaven to earth, earth to heaven. It gives to his prayer a particular structure.

His sanity recovered, Nebuchadnezzar's first movement is heavenward. To the three emotions of his soul ("I praised . . . I honored and glorified") he parallels three attributes of God (He lives forever, He dominates forever, He reigns forever) (verse 34). The three references to the eternity of God echo the three expressions of adoration by Nebuchadnezzar. Everything begins with the recognition of God's eternity, of His existence, of His dominion, and of His reign.

The resurrected one goes from death to life. Plunging back into existence, he is forever impressed with the notion of God's eternity. His prayer is then one of adoration, focused entirely on God. Nebuchadnezzar expresses his thankfulness (he praises God), his awe (he honors God), and his admiration (he glorifies God). As he emerges from insanity, Nebuchadnezzar sees nothing but God. He is suddenly aware that he owes Him everything. Without God he is nothing.

It is the first lesson he learns upon his return. "The peoples of the earth are regarded as nothing" (verse 35). The original text uses two words: *hshb,* which means "to evaluate," "to count," and *la,* which means "void," "nothingness," or the adverb of negation, "not." Next to God, the inhabitants of the earth seem like "nothing."

Salvation is then possible only through the miracle of creation. Nebuchadnezzar clearly alludes to creation in the classical association of "heaven and earth" with the "doing" and the "hand" of God (verse 35). In God's hand the armies of heaven as well as the inhabitants of the earth are powerless. "No one can hold back his hand or say to him: 'What have you done?'" It is an expression the Bible uses in the context of creation.

"Woe to him who quarrels with his Maker, to him who is but a potsherd among the potsherds on the ground. Does the clay say to the potter, 'What are you making?'" (Isa. 45:9).

"His wisdom is profound, his power is vast. . . . He speaks to the sun . . . ; he seals off the light of the stars. He alone stretches out the heavens and treads on the waves of the sea. He is the Maker of the

Bear. . . . Who can say to him, 'What are you doing?'" (Job 9:4-12).

It took the miracle of creation for Nebuchadnezzar to become whole. He had lost everything, including his own identity. Now he receives everything back: "My sanity was restored, my honor and splendor were returned to me" (Dan. 4:36). The word *tub* ("returned," "restored") appears three times in the passage, once in verse 34, twice in verse 36. He becomes even more prosperous: "I was restored to my throne and became even greater than before" (verse 36). In this sense, we can compare the king's experience to a resurrection. The resurrected one wakes up to life, coming forth from the tomb in a state even greater and more glorious than before (see 1 Cor. 15:35-50).

It is at the height of his success that the king pronounces the last words of his prayer, which are also his last words in the book of Daniel. The prayer ends as it had begun. The same threefold structure supports the divine attributes as well as the outpouring of his soul: "I, Nebuchadnezzar, praise and exalt and glorify the King of heaven" (Dan. 4:37). As opposed to the contented and prosperous "I, Nebuchadnezzar" of verse 4, this "I, Nebuchadnezzar" is entirely focused on heaven. The new king can now see beyond himself toward God. The picture of loving the God worthy of praise, honor, and glory is now completed with the dimension of justice: "Everything he does is right and all his ways are just. And those who walk in pride he is able to humble." Nebuchadnezzar has outgrown his naive pride. He has matured to humility. What others learn in a lifetime, Nebuchadnezzar has understood in seven years' time. Having experienced the precariousness of life, he knows now that he is not eternal. And aware of his limitations, he decides to follow the path of repentance and humility. The monarch has finally undergone conversion.

LITERARY STRUCTURE OF DANIEL 4

A   Hymnic confession (verses 1-3)
B   The dream (verses 4-33)
A₁ Hymnic confession (verses 34-37)

A   Hymnic confession (first person; verses 1-3)

B₁ Report of dream (first person; verses 4-18)

   a) Troubling dream

   b) The tree

   c) The heavenly watcher

B₂ Interpretation of dream (third person; verses 19-27)

   a) Troubling dream

   b) The tree

   c) The heavenly watcher

B₃ Fulfillment of dream (third person; verses 28-33)

   a) The king's pride

   b) The heavenly voice

   c) The king-ox

A₁ Hymnic confession (first person; verses 34-37)

---

[1] *Sanhedrin* 92b.

[2] Herodotus 1. 108.

[3] See S. Langdon, *Building Inscriptions of the Neo-Babylonian Empire* (1905), number 19: Wasi Brisa, B. Col. VII 34.

[4] See A. Barnes, *Notes on the Book of Daniel* (New York: 1881), p. 213.

[5] S. Birch, ed., *Records of the Past: Being English Translations of the Assyrian and Egyptian Monuments* (London: 1888-1892), vol. 7, p. 71.

[6] See S. Langdon, *Building Inscriptions of the Neo-Babylonian Empire* (Paris: 1905), Nebuchadnezzar, Nb. XIV, col. II, 39; see *Antiquities* 10. 223-226.

[7] See Albert Champdor, *Babylon,* trans. Elsa Coult (London/New York: 1958), p. 146.

[8] Cylindre de Grotefend, KB 3, 2, 39.

[9] In the Berlin Museum (cited in Francis D. Nichol, *The Seventh-day Adventist Bible Commentary* [Washington, D.C.: 1977], vol. 4, p. 799).

[10] See James A. Montgomery, *A Critical and Exegetical Commentary on the Book of Daniel* (New York: 1927), p. 244.

[11] 21:1 (Trad. Nau.).

[12] See especially M. Benezech et al, "A propos d'une observation de lycanthropie avec violences mortelles," in *Annales medico-psychologiques* 147, No. 4 (1989): 244.

[13] Gregory Zilboorg and George W. Henry, *A History of Medical Psychology* (New York: 1941), pp. 105, 167, 171, 228, 261.

[14] See J. P. Boulhaut, *Lycanthropie et pathologie mentale* (thesis, Université de Bordeaux II, 1988); cf. Ian Woodward, *The Werewolf Delusion* (New York: 1979), pp. 22-29.

[15] Harvey A. Rosenstock and Kenneth R. Vincent, "A Case of Lycanthropy," in *American Journal of Psychiatry* 134, No. 10 (1977): 1148.

[16] Josephus *Against Apion* 1. 146.

[17] Cited by Eusebius, in *Praeparatio Evangelica* 9. 11.

[18] A. K. Grayson, *Babylonian Historical-Literary Texts* (Toronto/Buffalo: 1975), pp. 87-92.

CHAPTER 5

THE HAND THAT MOVES

From the humble prayer of Nebuchadnezzar we next shift to the arrogant boasts of Belshazzar. The contrast is striking: Nebuchadnezzar is alone, barely emerging from the dust of his misery while Belshazzar sits upon his throne surrounded by a "thousand of his nobles," "drinking his wine" (Dan. 5:1, 2). Both pagan kings refuse the oracle predicting the end of Babylon. And both are forewarned by a prophecy that is then fulfilled as a judgment from God. Yet their destinies diverge. It almost seems as though Belshazzar deliberately took the opposite course to Nebuchadnezzar's.

Belshazzar was well acquainted with the great monarch who died, according to Babylonian chronicles, at the ripe old age of 104 in 562 B.C.E. By then Belshazzar was already 26 and head of the Babylonian army.[1] Our story takes place the evening before the capture of Babylon by Cyrus in 539 B.C.E., only about 20 years after the death of Nebuchadnezzar. Moreover, Belshazzar is, through his mother's lineage, the grandson of Nebuchadnezzar, a fact pointed out seven times by our chapter (verses 2, 11, 13, 18, 22). He had not forgotten his family history.

I. The King's Toast

In fact, the chapter opens on a Belshazzar who remembers his heritage. He orders his servants to bring to him the vases that Nebuchadnezzar had taken from the Temple in Jerusalem. But why precisely those vases? Because it is his intention to remake history. He is commemorating the victory of Babylon over Jerusalem, the triumph of the god of Babylon over the God of Israel: "As they drank the wine, they praised the gods of gold and silver, of bronze, iron, wood and stone" (verse 4).

They are the same metals as those of Nebuchadnezzar's statue and listed in the same order. The king's toast parodies his grandfather's dream. In chapter 2 the metals represented earthly kingdoms, bound to disappear. Now the king divinizes and adores them. Belshazzar has, through this gesture, deliberately and publicly emancipated himself from his grandfather.

But the mastermind behind Belshazzar's little show is in fact Nabonidus. One of the last Babylonian priests, he spent his lifetime trying to restore the ancient rites and sacred sites of the Babylonian cult Nebuchadnezzar had discarded. He was also Belshazzar's father. At the time of our story, Nabonidus is still alive and probably playing the role of invisible puppeteer. According to a Babylonian text,[2] Nabonidus, then residing in Tema (in the west), appointed his son as regent of Babylon, probably in 553 B.C.E. The opening scene of chapter 5 sees Belshazzar holding "a great banquet for a thousand of his nobles" (verse 1), a feast that turned out to be his last.

But Belshazzar is not just reacting against his grandfather. Behind the person of Nebuchadnezzar, it is God, the God of Israel, that he is provoking. Belshazzar resents this disturbing God. Feeling threatened by Him, he seeks to destroy a truth that torments him "by degrading what frightens him."[3] He does it not from conviction, but out of a sense of his own weakness and uncertainty. Like all religious crimes, it seeks the destruction of that which threatens to be the truth. It hopes to desacralize the sacred in an attempt to prove that it was never sacred in the first place.

Profaning the cult objects of the God of heaven is a way both to provoke God and to defy Him. Most often, God has met such challenges with silence. At times His lack of response almost seems to approve of history's tortures and inquisitions. In our story, however, God takes on the king's defiance.

II. Graffiti on the Wall

Suddenly, just above the lampstand, appears a hand! A hand that moves on its own, tracing its words on the white-washed wall (verse 5) in full view of the guests. Such precise details of the text are intentional. The vision did not go unnoticed. The king's face blanches and becomes as white as the wall. The scene turns to the grotesque. The noble silhouette of the king crumbles to a heap of bones rubbing against each other in fear: "His knees knocked together and his legs gave way" (verse 6). What was supposed to be a historical turning point became tragi-comedy. Helpless, the king yelps for his astrologers and diviners.

Its work done, the hand disappears. All that remains are the words it wrote. The king stares at them. Unfortunately, nobody understands the inscription. The confusion of the first scene leads to the dead silence of the astrologers, who also do not know. Belshazzar is now even more afraid (verse 9). He senses the déjà vu character of the scene as he remembers the experience of his grandfather Nebuchadnezzar. Only Daniel had then been capable of elucidating the dream. Could it be a manifestation of that same God?

III. The Queen's Reprimand

Enters then the queen. In ancient Middle Eastern culture, access to the court of the king was the privilege of only a few. No one dared enter the court without an official invitation, not even the king's spouse (see Esther 4:11, 16). In this case, the queen could not have been the king's wife—not with such in-depth knowledge about the era of Nebuchadnezzar's reign. Neither could she have been Belshazzar's mother, wife of Nabonidus, as the latter resided in distant Tema. As for the mother of Nabonidus, she had died in the ninth year of his reign (547 B.C.E.).[4] Indeed, the queen must be none other than the wife of Nebuchadnezzar himself, identified by Herodotus as the famous Nitocris.

As representative of her deceased husband, the queen mother received all due respect. She even enjoyed access to the royal court. The Bible attests to the importance of a queen mother, and of the significant role she played in politics (1 Kings 15:13; 2 Kings 11:1-3; 24:12; Jer. 13:18).

Seeing her, Belshazzar finds himself forced to remember what he had tried so hard to forget. Three times with the same phrase she exhorts him to remember: "In the time of your father . . . King Nebuchadnezzar your father—your father the king" (Dan. 5:11). Cutting deep into the king's suppressed memories, she draws out what haunted and disturbed Belshazzar most, forcing him to face the truth of Nebuchadnezzar's conversion, of his God, and of Daniel (verse 11).

IV. Belshazzar Consults Belteshazzar

Cornered by the queen, Belshazzar has no choice but to summon the ancient Hebrew prophet. He could have done so sooner. Daniel is still alive, and his reputation has not faded into oblivion, especially since he bears the same name as the king. If the king has not consulted Daniel, it is because he prefers to avoid him. Belshazzar is afraid of meeting with Belteshazzar. Interestingly, the king does not want to call him that name. Ignoring the prophet's Babylonian name, he refers to him by his Hebrew name. Belshazzar pretends he does not know his fellow namesake. His embarrassment dictates his hypocrisy.

But if Belshazzar seems to have forgotten Daniel and the religious experience of his grandfather, he manages to recall the prophet's origins: "Are you Daniel, one of the exiles my father the king brought from Judah?" (verse 13). His question recalls the wording of chapter 1 and seeks to remind Daniel and everyone else of the superiority of the Babylonian gods over the God of Israel. When he rephrases the words of the queen mother (verse 14), he carefully avoids the adjective "holy" she had used to qualify the God of Daniel. Belshazzar is manipulating the facts, omitting and recalling whatever will best serve his argument. He attempts to buy off Daniel by offering him a gold chain and a high position (verse 16). In essence, he is asking Daniel to distort the divine oracle, to say what the king wants to hear. He is also seeking the clemency of a God whom he seems to have angered.

V. Reprimand of a Prophet

Daniel's answer is stern. Accustomed as we are to Daniel's usual tact and respect, his harsh answer surprises us: "You may keep your gifts for yourself and give your rewards to someone else" (verse 17). Daniel has seen through the king and wants to maintain his own freedom of person and speech. But Daniel's anger does not result only from this latest incident. Belshazzar's wrong goes much deeper than his current silly bribery attempt. "But you his son, O Belshazzar, have not humbled yourself, though you knew all this" (verse 22).

We now understand Belshazzar, his attempt to bury the past and with it the God of Israel. Deep down, he knows and has always known the truth. And because it disturbs him, he seeks to destroy it, to forget it. He recognizes that the God of Israel is the true God, and it is his awareness that he attempts to smother through his forgetfulness. But Belshazzar has not forgotten—he consciously and openly rebels against a God in whom he believes: "Instead, you have set yourself up against the Lord of heaven" (verse 23). Indeed, the king is much more familiar with the Hebrew God than he cares to admit, a fact Daniel suggests at the end of his speech: "But you did not honor the God who holds in his hand your breath and all your ways" (verse 23, literal translation). The association of the "hand" and the "breath" clearly alludes to the creation of the first man, when God formed him with His hand (Ps. 119:73; Isa. 41:20) and breathed life into his nostrils (Gen. 2:7). It belongs to the biblical language of creation: "Which of all these does not know that the hand of the Lord has done this? In his hand is the life of every creature and the breath of mankind" (Job 12:9, 10; see also Job 34:14, 15; Ps. 104:28-30).

It is a Belshazzar, then, *who knows* (Dan. 5:22), who now discards the Creator for the idol of metal and of stone *which does not know* (verse 23). The first action generates the second. He who rejects the God of Creation will eventually fall back on idols, the work of his or her own hands and the image of one's own self. Such individuals become their own gods.

The role of prophet has taken precedence over that of the wise man. Instead of quickly deciphering the inscription, Daniel has let himself get sidetracked in a long accusatory speech. The underlying reason for the writing on the wall is what interests him more than the inscription itself. The king's salvation is more important than deciphering a mysterious message.

VI. The Decoding of the Graffiti

The elucidation of the mystery emerges out of Belshazzar's sin. The "hand" that appeared on the wall is none other than the hand that holds life: "But you did not honor the God who holds in his hand your life and all your ways. Therefore he sent the hand that wrote the inscription" (verses 23, 24). The king has two reasons to be afraid: first, because of the hand fluttering on the wall. Second, because it represents Him whom he had ignored and mocked. What Belshazzar perceives as a threat is but the outcome of his own sin. The first lesson that one gathers from the vision of the hand is that crime produces its own punishment.

But the hand left something behind: the inscription. In the Bible, when the hand of God writes, it generally does so in a context of judgment. The books written by God (Dan. 7:10; Ex. 31:18; 34:1; Rev. 3:5; 21:27), like the law engraved by the finger of God and placed in the ark of the covenant (Ex. 34:1; Deut. 10:5), form part of that judgment.[5]

Familiar with biblical thought, Belshazzar senses that the inscription brings such a judgment. Not only is it the hand of the Creator but also that of a judge. The Creator is judge. Only He who has woven the inner depths of the soul, who is able to grasp the most intimate thoughts, is in a position to judge. We understand now the biblical coupling of judgment and creation:

"O Lord, you have searched me and you know me. You know when I sit and when I rise; you perceive my thoughts from afar. . . . For you created my inmost being; you knit me together in my mother's womb. . . . My frame was not hidden from you. . . . Search me, O God, and know my heart; test me and know my anxious thoughts" (Ps. 139:1-23; see Rev. 14:7).

The writing on the wall now terrifies Belshazzar. He knows that it is a message from the Creator, the divine judge. Somehow he must find a way to find its meaning. But that is not an easy task.

The first difficulty resides in the fact that the Aramaic text uses no vowels, as is the case with many ancient inscriptions. To read such a text, one must already be familiar with its meaning. "Whoever reads this writing and tells me what it means . . ." (Dan. 5:7). The fact that there may have been also no separation between words makes the deciphering all the more difficult. To give you an idea of what the astrologers were up against, here is the English equivalent of the text, with no vowels and no separation between words: NMBRDNMBRDWGDNDDVDD. We can understand the Chaldeans' failure. Only a revelation from its author would make it possible to read it, let alone to understand. In any case, even with the vowels, the words made no sense.

"MENE, MENE, TEKEL, UPHARSIN." On a first level of interpretation, we are dealing with measures of weight. *Mene* (the mina, 600 g.), *Tekel* (the shekel, 10 g.), *Upharsin* (a half mina, 300 g.). It was a message any street vendor at the marketplace could have shouted to inform his clientele of the different weight values of his merchandise. Belshazzar gets the hint: it is a liquidation of stock sale and therefore the end of his business. Belshazzar was quite familiar with such commercial jargon. History tells us that neo-Babylonian kings, in addition to their administrative functions, made commercial transactions.[6] In Babylon buying and selling were the national pastime. Not only was Belshazzar king of Babylon, he was also a reputed wool merchant. With his commercial background, the writing on the wall should have been clear to him. Daniel will be even more explicit, going back to the etymology of each word, according to the biblical method of interpretation.[7]

Mene derives from a root that means "to count," "to assign," "to determine." Its root also appears in chapter 1 in reference to the daily amount of food the king "assigned" (verse 5). This word occurs in the Bible only in relation to the Creator, who controls and determines the flow of history. The root of the word *Mene* also designates the Babylonian god of destiny, "Meni" (Isa. 65:11, 12). Arabic understands the derivative *manye* in the sense of "fatality" or "destiny." The divine message compares Belshazzar to merchandise that is "determined," that is, to be liquidated. The king's fate awaits him (Dan. 5:26).

Tekel comes from a root meaning "to weigh," another image pertaining to the commercial world. Belshazzar is here "weighed on the scales" (verse 27). And like a common piece of merchandise, his weight has been "found wanting" (NIV has the literal translation of *hassir*). In other words, he is a fraud. We are in a juridical context, as the weighing and the scales infer. For the Bible, and ancient Middle Eastern culture as a whole, it is also the language of God's judgment.[8]

"For the Lord is a God who knows, and by him deeds are weighed" (1 Sam. 2:3).

"Let God weigh me in honest scales" (Job 31:6).

Belshazzar is well aware of the connotation of judgment and condemnation implied by the words of the message.

Upharsin derives from a root meaning "to break up," "to shatter." The word occurs often in the Bible in a context of violence. "And break *[prs]* their bones in pieces" (Micah 3:3). In Hebrew, the white-tailed eagle, a bird of prey, is *peres* (Deut. 14:12) because it tears everything apart *(prs)*. The divine message compares Belshazzar to merchandise that falls prey to foreigners and gets torn into pieces. It is something already hinted at in the plural form of the word *upharsin*, the only plural of the inscription, implying simultaneously a plurality of predators, the Medes and the Persians. Already the sound of the word *prs* alludes to the Persians. Belshazzar knows now that his kingdom has come to an end.

The idea of termination permeates each word. *Mene* (numbered) is the end of the stock; *Tekel* (weighed) implies a lack or a degeneration; and *Upharsin* (and divided) the idea of dissolution. But beyond the words themselves, in their rhythm, one can hear the four fatal chimes of the end. The inscription consists of four words made possible by the intentional repetition of the word *Mene*. And to each word Daniel adds a four-word explanation in Aramaic.

Text of the inscription: four words

Explanation of *Mene:* four words

Explanation of *Tekel:* four words

Explanation of *Upharsin:* four words[9]

The number four plays a prominent role in the book of Daniel. The statue of Nebuchadnezzar consisted of four metals, representing the succession of four kingdoms until the end. The same four kingdoms will appear in Daniel 7 in the form of four beasts. Extrabiblical literature also observes this cycle of four. The ancient oracles of Persia and Babylon[10] often speak of a cycle of four kingdoms, without necessarily implying the four kingdoms of the book of Daniel. There is no fifth kingdom. Earthly kingdoms do not exceed four. The number four is the omen of the end.

For Belshazzar, the allusion hits home. Four kings succeed Nebuchadnezzar: Amel-Marduk (562-560),[11] Neriglissar (560-556),[12] Labashi-Marduk (556), and finally Nabonidus (556-539), with Belshazzar as the regent. There will not be any more kings. Belshazzar understands he is the last Neo-Babylonian monarch.

V. The King's Death

The rhythm of the story picks up. The king reacts "immediately" (literal translation of Dan. 5:29), having no other choice. After hurriedly honoring Daniel, he then brushes him aside to tend to more urgent matters, such as the approaching enemy army. The text ends on an ironic note: having lost everything, Belshazzar is now willing to share all that he has, even his kingly prerogatives. The king's attendants drape Daniel in a purple mantle, the royal color (cf. Esther 8:15),[13] and Belshazzar appoints him third man of the kingdom, after Nabonidus and himself. As for the gold chain, it is a token of great honor.

Daniel now accepts the presents, knowing that the upcoming events will nullify their value. Within hours the prophecy is fulfilled. Invading forces occupy Babylon and murder Belshazzar in the process. A new king, Darius the Mede, ascends to the throne.

Among the cuneiform documents relating the fall of Babylon, the "chronicle of Nabonidus" testifies to the accuracy of the biblical story: "Gobryas *(Ugbaru),* the governor of Gutium and the army of Cyrus entered Babylon without battle. Afterward Nabonidus was arrested in Babylon when he returned. . . . In the month of Arahshamnu, the third day, Cyrus entered in Babylon. . . . Gobryas, his governor, installed (sub-)governors in Babylon."[14] The Babylonian text does not mention Belshazzar, since its main focus is on Nabonidus. But the latter's absence confirms the existence of a regent prince in Babylon.

The first thing the new governor does is to appoint regents under him, something also mentioned in the book of Daniel (Dan. 6:3). Evidence suggests that Gobryas is none other than Darius the Mede. The name Darius is an honorary title meaning "he who holds the scepter," and Gobryas could well have adopted it.

According to ancient chronicles, Gobryas died a year and three weeks after the fall of Babylon, thus explaining why Cyrus did not take the title of "king of Babylon" until a year later,[15] and why Daniel 6:28 mentions him as the immediate successor of Darius. Otherwise known as Darius the Mede, Gobryas is 62 at the beginning of his rule (Dan. 5:31) and reigned for just a year over Babylon. And indeed, the book of Daniel only alludes to the first year of his reign (Dan. 9:1).

Chapter 5 constitutes a turning point in the book of Daniel: the kingdom of the Medes and Persians succeeds that of Babylon in partial fulfillment of the prophecy in chapter 2. Like his grandfather (chapter 3), Belshazzar sought to escape the truth, tenaciously maintaining that Babylon was eternal. Both monarchs would be reminded of their temerity by violent intervention from above. The tree would be cut down, and the hand would claim back the breath. Both verified in their existence the fulfillment of the prophetic words. Likewise, the remaining predicted events would also come to pass. In the person of Belshazzar, both prophecies would find their fulfillment: the ancient prophecy of the statue, as well as the most recent one written on the wall.

STRUCTURE OF DANIEL 5

A The king's glory (verses 1-4)
    B The mystery of the writing (verses 5-9)
        C The queen's sermon (verses 10-12)
           D Belshazzar consults Belteshazzar (verses 13-16)
        C_1 The prophet's sermon (verses 17-24)
    B_1 The deciphering of the writing (verses 25-28)
A_1 The fall of the king (verses 29-31)

---

[1] Birch, *Records of the Past,* vol. 7, p. 159.

[2] Pritchard, *Ancient Near Eastern Texts,* p. 313.

[3] Lacocque, *The Book of Daniel,* p. 94.

[4] Pritchard, pp. 306, 560, 561.

[5] Also in the New Testament, Jesus traces in the dust a judgment against the accusers of the adulterer (John 8:6).

[6] See Theophilus G. Pinches, *The Old Testament: In the Light of the Historical Records and Legends of Assyria and Babylonia* (London: 1903), pp. 430-451.

[7] See Micah 1; Jer. 7:11; Amos 8:1.

[8] Compare the many Egyptian bas reliefs that depict the god Anubis leading the deceased toward a great scale that will weigh the person's heart before the goddess Maat.

[9] The two words "Medes and Persians" are counted as one unit, since they stand for a single kingdom.

[10] Pritchard, pp. 606, 607.

[11] Called Evil-Merodach in Scripture (2 Kings 25:27; Jer. 52:31-34).

[12] Nergal-Sharezer in Scripture (Jer. 39:3, 13).

[13] Xenophon *Anabasis* (1. 2, 5, etc.).

[14] Pritchard, p. 306.

[15] See William H. Shea, "An Unrecognized Vassal King of Babylon in the Early Achaemenid Period," *Andrews University Seminary Studies* 10 (1972): 113-117.

LIONS UNDER A CHARM

Chapter 6 starts where chapter 5 left off. Darius has ascended the throne, and Daniel has just been promoted. We are in 539 B.C.E. Life is good for the exiled prince.

But will it last? We remember the peaceful days of the last part of chapter 2. There also, the three Hebrews received promotions. But the honors only set them up for the ordeal in chapter 3. Will history repeat itself? The author of the book of Daniel seems to imply so. Chapter 6 parallels chapter 3, with the same development, the same wordings, and the same phrases ("to set up," "to accuse," "with haste," "decree," etc.). Likewise, the repetition of key words inside the chapter itself ("king," "Daniel," "kingdom," "pray," "lion," "den," etc.) echoes the repetition of the officials and of the musical instruments in chapter 3. Such a stylistic procedure suggests that Daniel is now going through the same experience as the three Hebrews of chapter 3. The absence of the three Hebrews in this context, as well as the absence of Daniel in chapter 3, does not result from cowardice. Had they found themselves in the same circumstances, their reaction would have been the same. Events now restrict themselves to a higher administrative level, involving only Daniel.

I. The Babel Complex

As in chapter 3, the main concern at the opening of chapter 6 is to build a strong basis for the kingdom. And as before, the king summons the high officials. In chapter 3 the issue concerned the "setting up" *(hqm)* of the statue (verse 1). The main concern of our present chapter focuses on the "setting up" *(hqm)* of administrators over the kingdom (Dan. 6:1). The same Aramaic verb appears in both chapters.

Right from the start Daniel finds himself set apart from his colleagues. The administration was shared among 120 satraps, or governors (see Esther 1:1; 8:9).[1] Above the governors were three presidents. Daniel is one of them. The king even considers setting him *(hqm)* over the whole kingdom (Dan. 6:3).

Darius intends to build his administrative success on Daniel. Several reasons inspire his choice. First of all, the Hebrew is, like him, a foreigner, an ally in a strange land. Daniel also predicted the fall of Babylon and the succession of the Medo-Persian kingdom. Moreover, the prophet had just been appointed governor of the kingdom and has served the country for many years. To avoid further chaos, Darius decides to leave the main structures of the Babylonian government intact. But the real reason is not political. "Daniel so distinguished himself among the administrators and the satraps by his exceptional qualities that the king planned to set him over the whole kingdom" (verse 3). Daniel 5:12 and chapters 1 and 2 refer to the same "superiority" to describe God's blessing and inspiration. In other words, the king is seeking to appropriate and exploit the extraordinary power Daniel possessed. The Babel mentality infiltrates itself even into the king's good intentions. We are again in a religious context, and it is in this light that we should interpret the rest of the passage.

II. When Daniel Is Praying

The behavior of the satraps echoes that of the Chaldeans toward the three Hebrews (chapter 3). Interestingly, it contains all the characteristics of modern anti-Semitism: the same hatred of foreigners, their customs, and their religion; the same morbid jealousy; the same allusion to a Jewish origin (Dan. 6:13); and the same political concern. Where society perceives the Jew as a threat to unity, anti-Semitism becomes the unifying factor of nations and ideologies, whether it be Marxism or Nazism, left-wing tendencies or right-wing ones.

Chapter 6 offers a lesson for the majority, warning them not only against the temptation of anti-Semitism, but also against any form of xenophobic oppression. Whether it be a Jew in a Christian setting, or a Black in a White neighborhood, anti-Semitism is the prototype of the hatred between races, religions, and nations—the hatred of the difference. Anti-Semitism is a crime against humanity, but it does so in disguise. In the name of the state, of God, or of Allah, we despise, we pursue, and we crucify. Anti-Semitism is essentially religious. We hate and kill with a clear conscience, certain of God's approval and blessing. The story of Daniel uncovers the hidden mechanism of anti-Semitism. The religion of the satraps is a human production. Instead of being inspired from above, it emerges from an administrative committee: "The royal administrators, prefects, satraps, advisers and governors have all agreed that the king should issue an edict" (verse 7). They program adoration, and disobedience automatically results in death in the lions' den. Their decision made, they now rush to the king "as a group" (verses 6, 11, 15). Everything depends on their own political performance, hence the surge of nervous activity. Workaholicism is a symptom of a godless age. The obsession with success that we sometimes encounter in our religious communities is not necessarily a sign of holiness, but betrays rather a disconnection from God.

The human has replaced God, a substitution described in legal terms: the law of God, *dat* (verse 5), has been discarded for human law, *dat* (verse 8). The same word *qayam* characterizes both the human decree (verses 7, 15) and that from the God of heaven (verse 26). This hypocrisy, this voiding of God that pretends to be God, is the root of all fanaticism and intolerance. And indeed, its adherents will enforce the royal decree with violence: "Anyone who prays to any god or man during the next thirty days, except to you, O king, shall be thrown into the lions' den" (verse 7).

The violence hurled against the "unbeliever" is but the symptom of the persecutor's religious failure. From the Crusades to the Inquisition, from Hitler to Stalin to the ayatollahs, there always appears the same pattern of intolerance. When a religion poses as an absolute, convinced that it is *the* truth, it cannot stand the sight of other religions, perhaps because they may remind it too much of its own presumptions and lies.

But the godly believer does not worry. The contrast, as depicted in chapter 6, between Daniel and the crowd around him is striking. Surrounded by the noisy satraps, he remains silent. He turns neither to his colleagues nor to the king. Instead, he withdraws to his room and faces the west. To political strategy, Daniel opposes prayer.

It is the fifth prayer in the book of Daniel. The context is one of despair. The aged prophet knows he is powerless. Acquainted with Median and Persian law, he realizes that once a decree is issued, it is irrevocable (verse 8). A similar example of the principle appears in the book of Esther (Esther 8:8). Extrabiblical literature contains the case of a man sentenced to death for a crime that he did not commit. When his innocence was finally proven, it was too late to revoke the edict, and the man was executed.[2] Daniel saw no way out. Even the king could do nothing. The prophet's prayer takes on new significance when seen in such a context. He does not offer it as a religious duty, nor out of routine or superstition. Nor does it attempt to dress itself with oratorical beauty. Such a prayer is rare, for it arises from the threat of imminent death and presents only the essential.

But in many ways the prayer is no different than Daniel's previous ones. It is not the circumstances that have forced him into this state of prayer. The text mentions that he "prayed, . . . just as he had done before" (verse 10). To the religious lockstep of the satraps, Daniel opposes the prayer of a free man. He prays no matter what the circumstances, in good times and in bad. Prayer is not for him a last resort for sickness or in death, but an integral part of his life. The prayer of Daniel is that of a hero *and* of a saint.

It takes heroic courage to ignore the edict and to pray anyway. In performing the simple act of kneeling, Daniel risks his life. He could have prayed in secret. Scripture even encourages prayer in seclusion (Matt. 6:6). When prayer becomes trendy, it is better to pray alone. But when the authorities outlaw prayer, to pray in hiding is to imply that the king is greater than God. Daniel could have, for a while at least, adapted to the circumstances. After all, God forgives—He knows a person's heart. But Daniel prefers to die rather than to put a momentary hold on his religious life. Under these overcast skies, he does not run for shelter, but stands tall as a free man. The prophet chooses to remain faithful to God in his heart *and* in his actions. His courage is remarkable. An intelligent and experienced man, Daniel knows what he is up against. It is not the action of naive virtue, incapable of anticipating the gravity of the consequences.

But more than the prayer of a hero, Daniel's prayer is that of a saint. It is easier to say a prayer in the midst of trouble than in daily life. To the courage of Daniel we must add the virtue of patience. "It is easier to be a hero than a saint," Dr. Rieux comments in Albert Camus' novel *The Plague*. A heroic gesture is short-lived and public. This is what makes it heroic. A saintly action, on the other hand, remains in obscurity and lasts a lifetime. Nobody applauds, nobody knows or cares. It takes less effort to pray during an emergency or trial than in the course of ordinary life.

If Daniel does not succumb to his ordeal, it is because of the frame he gave to his prayer. In his house he set apart an "upstairs room" for his daily prayer, a luxury only a few very high-ranking officials had (2 Kings 1:2; 4:10, 11). Prayer becomes, then, associated with a place, making it easier to leave other concerns on its threshold. Also, Daniel maintained his prayer life through discipline. The prophet prays "three times a day" (Dan. 6:10, 13). Prayer should not depend only upon those "stirrings of the soul" that come and go according to our mood or the quality of the moonlight. The example of Daniel teaches us that we must integrate prayer into the rhythm of life itself. Prayer *is* life. It must be nourished, it must be tended to, it must be allowed to breathe. A sigh, a longing of the soul, prayer is a basic need that we must perform even when the feeling is not there. Our prayer life must be as much a part of us as meals, work, and other appointments. Only then will we be strong enough to face the ordeal when it comes.

Interestingly, Daniel's time of prayer coincides with the schedule of the sacrifices in the Temple of Jerusalem (1 Chron. 23:30-31). In remembrance of these rituals, Daniel faces west. During his prayer inaugurating the Temple, Solomon already sensed this extrapolation from ritual to the prayer of the exiled. "And if they have a change of heart in the land where they are held captive . . . if they . . . pray to you toward the . . . city you have chosen and the temple I have built for your Name; then from heaven, your dwelling place, hear their prayer" (1 Kings 8:47-49).

Prayer is thus intimately linked to the sacrifices. Like the sacrifice, God intends for prayer to bring us nearer to Him. The Hebrew verb "to sacrifice" comes from the root *qrb,* which means "near" and implies God's approach to the person. Prayer is not the ascension of human beings to God, but the descent of God to humanity. Here lies the difference between Daniel's religion and that of the Babylonians, who depended on their own efforts.

The orientation of the prayer toward the Temple is also a gesture of hope: the hope of the exiled for return, for the restoration of the Temple. Prayer also holds the dimension of the future. Daniel does not turn toward Jerusalem like a sorcerer who would turn to the sky for rain. His gesture has no magical purpose. He knows the answer to his problem lies elsewhere—"in heaven," as Solomon said. Daniel prays toward Jerusalem because he hopes in the future. His prayer is situated in time, not in space. For the Hebrew, the sacred lies in time, not in space. It is not the monument that matters, but the time. Abraham Heschel observed that "'the day of the Lord' is more important to the prophets than 'the house of the Lord.'"[3]

The three monotheistic religions—Judaism, Christianity, and Islam—have retained Daniel's gesture. All three religions would orient their prayers and build their places of worship in the direction of Jerusalem.

Daniel's prayer weaves itself around the two elements of faith and hope implied by two verbs. Daniel "gives thanks" (Dan. 6:10), and he "asks" (verse 11). The first verb comes from the word *yad* (open hand) and expresses the gratitude of someone who has received something. The second word, *mithannan,* derives from *hnn* (grace) and is the supplication of the person who has not received.

Prayer then has its roots in deprivation and blossoms in the grace of a God who gives. To pray is to recognize one's own void and to acknowledge that all that is comes from above. Such prayer is an act of humility. Daniel kneels to pray, the gesture of the slave or of the vanquished soldier whose destiny now rests in the hands of the master.

III. In the Lions' Den

But the prayer of Daniel goes unheard. God Himself seems powerless. Events follow their course, and Daniel stands condemned. Darius musters a few words of encouragement: "May your God, whom you serve continually, rescue you!" (Dan. 6:16), the same expression used by the three Hebrews in response to Nebuchadnezzar (Dan. 3:17). But the words carry no weight. Guards throw Daniel into the den and seal the door. According to Herodotus, a strong rope bound the stone door. It had also a patch of clay on which the king would apply his seal (Dan. 6:17).[4] Daniel's destiny is sealed. A veil of silence now falls over the scene.

The king goes to bed without eating (verse 18). In ancient times the evening meal was the most important of the day (Ex. 16:8). After the hot day, it was the ideal moment for invitations and dinner parties. The king's abstinence is more than the expression of his sadness—it is a fast. Middle Eastern culture, as does the biblical tradition, associates fasting with prayer (Dan. 10:3). Powerless, the king turns as a last resort to religious supplication. The next morning he rushes to the lion pit to see if his prayer has been answered. With anguish in his voice, he speaks: "Daniel, servant of the living God, has your God, whom you serve continually, been able to rescue you from the lions?" (Dan. 6:20).

The aged prophet replies calmly, "O king, live forever!" (verse 21). To the "living God" *(hay)* of the king echoes Daniel's "live forever" *(hay)*. The life of the king answers to the life of God. There is a biological dependence between the two. If the king is "alive," it is because of the "living" God. Likewise, if Daniel is alive, it is because of that same living God. Daniel makes no allusion to his great courage, nor to his outstanding faith. He prefers to center his testimony on the living God, who has "shut the mouths of the lions" (verse 22).

Again, as in chapter 3, salvation comes from above as God sends an angel. Beyond our power, salvation has its origin outside of ourselves. Daniel is not rescued by his own wisdom, nor by a superior display of courage, but "because he had trusted in his God" (verse 23). Faith saves him.

Daniel was innocent (verse 22), but that was not enough to rescue him. He needed faith for God to send the angel.

But faith does not exclude justice. Though salvation is from God alone, faith cannot survive without works, without a response in deed and action. It is because Daniel has faith in God that he remains innocent. Religion is more than just "believing" in God's salvation—it is "living" and fighting in the present with God's help. People have often relegated religion to the abstract level of fleshless dogma frosted with beautiful emotions. Daniel's experience gives us the example of an incarnated religion for everyday life with its efforts and uncertainties.

IV. The Revenge

The two orders the king gave at the beginning of our story have their echo in two more that he now issues. The command to throw Daniel into the den has its counterpart in the decree to throw the prophet's accusers along with their whole families into the den. But it is as pointless as the first one. Violence for God does not atone for violence against God. Darius remains as obtuse as ever as he prefers to follow the custom.[5] The punishment is collective so as to avoid possible retaliation from surviving family members. This time no angel intervenes. The lions do not even give their victims time to hit the ground. According to a tradition recorded by Flavius Josephus,[6] Daniel's accusers would have questioned the authenticity of the miracle by suggesting that the lions had been so well fed that they ignored Daniel. They now receive an up-close chance to test their objection.

The edict to adore the God of Daniel replaces the edict to adore the king. The decree of Darius parallels that of Nebuchadnezzar in chapter 3. But whereas Nebuchadnezzar had forbidden only slander against God, Darius orders that people adore Him: "I issue a decree that in every part of my kingdom people must fear and reverence the God of Daniel" (verse 26).

Darius realizes the universal aspect of the lion den miracle. When one encounters the reality of God's existence, it is impossible to remain silent. His decree hence glorifies the living God. *The sixth prayer in the book of Daniel,* it reminds us of Nebuchadnezzar's prayer in chapter 4 through its similarities of style, words, and content. The prayer also centers on God and on His eternal kingdom. But Darius has a deeper understanding of the Hebrew God than did Nebuchadnezzar, as we see when he confesses God as the "living God," the Creator and Saviour. His first words describe Him as the eternally "living God" who "endures forever" and whose "kingdom will not be destroyed" like the earthly kingdoms (verse 26).

The Persian king's prayer builds on the theme of life. Through prayer one becomes more aware of genuine life that endures and in which happiness is more than a mirage. Prayer is an act of protest against suffering and death, a cry against the unacceptable. Through prayer we receive hope. To pray is to love life, to be bound again to life through God. Such prayer is the realization that without God nothing could exist or survive. In the morning we pray as we wake up to daily life. At noon we pray for the bread that sustains us. And in the evening we surrender our souls to His keeping.

The theme of life celebrated by prayer is rooted in the biblical event of Creation. Life is related to God because He is its source, the Creator of all that is. This is where biblical prayer differs from pagan prayer. Pagans pray to what they have made. Bible believers pray to Him who made them. That is why prayer addresses the invisible. Any depiction of God is human-made, thus falsifying the prayer. People then perceive everything in the universe as "signs and wonders" (verse 27). The sun and the stars, the mountains and the sea, man and woman, sprang up neither on their own initiative or by chance. All resulted from intentional creation. And all is a miracle, a sign of the invisible God. The act of prayer has its roots in the event of Creation. It is the faith that God has the power to transform misery into joy, death into life, nothing into something.

Only in this context can salvation intervene as we see in the third statement of the prayer: "He rescues and he saves" (verse 27). Belief in salvation implies belief in Creation, and belief in Creation mandates belief in the living God. For only the Creator who is still alive has the power to change death into life. Prayer is more than a comforting and subjective experience. It aspires to a change of cosmic dimensions. More than a transcendental experience of harmony and peace, it is an existential outcry for a better world. When we pray for our daily bread, for the sick, and even for world peace, the quest is always the same. The ultimate fulfillment of prayer is salvation, the coming of the kingdom of God. The ancient rabbis used to say that "a prayer, wherein there is not mention of the kingdom of God, is not a prayer."[7] That is why the ultimate outcome of prayer is resurrection. The three ideas contained in the prayer of Darius (the "living God," the Creator God, and the God who saves) converge in the event of resurrection: "He has rescued Daniel from the power of the lions" (verse 27).

The three themes of life, creation, and salvation were already present in Daniel's experience. Surviving the lions and emerging out of the den unharmed, as had the three Hebrews in chapter 3, Daniel is considered as risen from the dead. In the New Testament the Epistle to the Hebrews remembers both stories and interprets them in the light of resurrection (Heb. 11:33, 34). The biblical tradition, especially the Psalms, often uses the lion to symbolize the power of death (Ps. 22:13, 21; 57:4-6; 91:9-13). Christian imagery has also retained this story as a symbol of victory over death. Believers have depicted the scene of Daniel saved from the lions on sarcophagi as a reminder in death of the miracle of resurrection.[8] In a Christian perspective, the story of Daniel presents many similarities to the story of Jesus, a point already acknowledged by the early Christians, for whom the book of Daniel became a constant source of inspiration.[9] Like Daniel, Jesus was the victim of a plot by high-placed officials jealous of His influence. As in the story of Daniel, evil forces manipulated the ruling authority and invoked a political reason to justify the sentence. In both cases the victim was innocent, and attempts to save him are made in vain. And in both cases resurrection occurs from a sealed tomb.

Daniel emerges from the dead greater than before. He is free. The God condemned to be adored in hiding, considered a mere tribal deity, is now God of the universe (Dan. 6:26, 27). Everything is reversed. The victory of Daniel is resounding. It warns the opportunists who stoop to the gods of success, and it encourages the rare few who still choose the risk of faith.

V. Daniel's Success

The end of the story mentions Daniel's success in parallel to the three Hebrews' success in chapter 3. But where the prosperity of the three Hebrews resulted from the king (Dan. 3:30), Daniel's prosperity remains independent of royal clemency and continues right on through the reign of Cyrus. The chapter ends on a note of hope that transcends the prophet's personal happiness and the miracle itself. The mention of "Cyrus the Persian" (verse 28) already hints at the end of the Exile as the fulfillment of the prophecies concerning Israel's restoration.

In the book of Daniel the name "Cyrus" is in fact a point of reference. "Cyrus" marks the conclusion of the first chapter, but also occurs near the end of the whole book (Dan. 10:1). It surfaces now in the conclusion of the first part of the book of Daniel. The two parts are thus clearly outlined by its occurrence.

The first part is the story of Daniel—of his life, of his ordeals and success. The prophetic dreams of this section for the most part confine themselves to the lifetimes of the persons involved. In the second part, however, we leave the contemporary scene for the "distant future" (Dan. 8:26; 12:4, 9). Both parts are interrelated. Each one confirms the other. Witnessing the fulfillment of past prophecies encourages us to believe in the authenticity and eventual fulfillment of future ones. The miracle encountered in daily life is the sign of another reality: "His kingdom will not be destroyed" (Dan. 6:26; 4:3, 34). The experience of God in everyday life nourishes the dream for still another kingdom. This is the intent behind divine intervention: to strengthen faith and hope and to kindle our longing for a new world.

The first part of the book has prepared the way for the second part.

STRUCTURE OF DANIEL 6
(Cf. Chapter 3)

A   Daniel's success (verses 1-3)

    B   The satraps' accusation (verses 4-13)

        C   The lions (verses 14-24)

- Dialogue
- Daniel cast in the den
- Dialogue
- Daniel saved from the den

    B₁   The revenge (verses 25-27)

A₁   Daniel's success (verse 28)

---

[1] See also Herodotus 3. 89.

[2] Diodorus of Sicily 17. 30.

[3] Abraham J. Heschel, *The Sabbath: Its Meaning for Modern Man* (New York: 1951), p. 79.

[4] Herodotus 1. 195.

[5] Herodotus 3. 119.

[6] *Antiquities* 10.

[7] Babylonian Talmud *Berakoth* 40b.

[8] M. Delcor, *Le Livre de Daniel* (Paris: 1971), pp. 138, 139.

[9] Aphrahat, *Demonstrations in Nicene and Post-Nicene Fathers* (Grand Rapids: 1989), vol. 13, p. 399.

FOUR BEASTS AND
A SON OF MAN

We are now in the middle of the book of Daniel. Commentators have called the seventh chapter the "heart,"[1] the "veritable centre"[2] of the book of Daniel. It is the pivot that begins the second part of the book. From now on, history does not take the form of actual events anymore. Instead we dimly perceive it from afar through a dream or vision. The style switches from the concrete to the symbolic. We encounter bizarre animals and obscure numbers, a genre termed "apocalyptic." To mark the transition, the author interrupts the chronological flow of events.

Chapter 7 brings us back to the time of Belshazzar, when Nabonidus was still in Tema[3] (553 B.C.E). It is also the year of Cyrus's victory over the king of the Medes, Astyages.

In spite of its obscurity, chapter 7 has a number of familiar motifs taken from the preceding chapters, especially chapter 2. In fact, the two visions follow a parallel development. They cover the same time span, from Babylon to the end of human time, and evoke the same four kingdoms represented symbolically by metals in chapter 2, and by beasts in chapter 7. Such a parallel is more than a unifying factor—it is the key to our method of interpretation. We must read chapter 7 in the light of chapter 2.

The two visions remain, however, distinct. In chapter 2 Nebuchadnezzar received the vision. Here a dream visits Daniel himself. The link between the content of the dream and its communication is more direct as we already see implied by a play on words: "Daniel had a dream, and visions passed through his mind [*resh*] as he was lying on his bed. He wrote down the substance [*resh*] of his dream" (Dan. 7:1).

Through this echo of the word *resh,* the author establishes a direct link between what has been revealed and what has been recorded. In other words, we are not allowed any room for embellishment. What God revealed is what the author will narrate—no more and no less. And because God presented it, we should take it seriously.

From the start, the vision functions on a universal level. It is churned up from water and framed by the four winds of the earth (verse 2). The mention of water sends us back to the time of Creation (Gen. 1:1), and the four winds of the earth personify the four corners of the earth (Zech. 6:5, 6). The prophecy of Daniel concerns the whole world.

We can break the vision into three successive scenes, each introduced by the same expression: "In my vision at night I looked" (Dan. 7:2, 7, 13). The interjection "and there," *waaru* (verses 2, 5, 7, 13) or *waalu* (verse 8) divides each scene in turn into subparts.

I. The Lion, the Bear, and the Leopard

In reality, the beasts of the vision only remotely resemble the animals we usually compare them to: "The first beast was like" (verses 4-6). The scene is almost surrealistic, an incoherent collage of familiar elements. In any case, it presents all the characteristics of a nightmare.

But in the historical context of the time, the mention of such animals carries great meaning. In the Babylonian tradition animals symbolize upcoming historical events. But in biblical tradition such hybrid types violate the principle of creation that each animal be "according to its kind" (Gen. 1) as well as the Levitical law: "Do not mate different kinds of animals" (Lev. 19:19). The animals therefore represent malevolent or evil forces.

1. The Lion

The winged lion corresponds to the first metal of the statue in Daniel 2 and represents Babylon. It is not necessary to unearth mythological and astrological traditions in order to justify its relationship to Babylon. Biblical sources as well as Babylonian sculpture will suffice. Indeed, Babylonian art often depicts winged lions, as we see, for example, on the glazed tile walls preserved in various museums. A great many winged lions decorated the main road to Babylon. Interestingly, Scripture represents Nebuchadnezzar himself by the double image of the lion and the eagle (Jer. 49:19, 22).

But the metaphor of the winged lion has even more to it, as it couples the strength of the lion (Prov. 30:30) with the speed of the eagle (2 Sam. 1:23). He becomes almost invincible. This kingdom is the best, just like the first kingdom that chapter 2 described as the "head" and the "king of kings." As for the tearing off of the wings, they remind us of the ripping off of the branches of the great tree of chapter 4. The beast is then lifted up from the ground and made to stand on two feet like a man. In the book of Daniel human characteristics render the religious dimension (see our commentary on "the clay" in chapter 2). In an allusion to Nebuchadnezzar's recovery and conversion, he receives the heart of a man. The vertical position symbolizes the king now able to be moved by God, the forces pulling the beast down on all fours having been momentarily defeated. This conversion of a pagan king to the God of Israel, still fresh in Daniel's memory from some 10 years before, is extraordinary and deserves, therefore, a special mention. The mystery of the winged lion is then easy to solve: it represents Babylon. But the winds of change draw out yet another monster.

2. The Bear

From this kingdom on, the beasts do not reflect the historical and cultural contexts of each kingdom, but rather a function of their psychology. Looking up horoscope manuals or ancient myths will not help us understand the imagery. The Bible characterized the bear by its cruelty (2 Sam. 17:8; Prov. 28:15; Amos 5:19). The parallel passage of Daniel 2 identifies the bear with the Medes and Persians, a conclusion confirmed by the bear's bizarre posture: "It was raised up on one of its sides" (Dan. 7:5). The creature is evidently not standing on its hind paws, because it is later told to "get up and eat." More likely the bear has raised on one of its sides, left or right, presenting one part of its body as higher than the other and ready to strike. It is a "lopsidedness" already hinted at by the *haphel* form of the Aramaic "raised." The image of the "side," biblical symbol of aggressiveness (see Eze. 34:21, which describes the aggressiveness of the sheep that shoves "with flank and shoulder"), alludes to the creature's cruelty. In chapter 8 two horns, one bigger than the other (verse 3), depict the power of the Medes and Persians. A bear "raised up on one of its sides" thus represents a duality of powers, one stronger than the other.

History confirms the prophetic picture. Around 650 B.C.E. the Persians were the vassals of the Medes, though they had autonomy and conducted their own governmental affairs. In the 550s Cyrus, son of the Persian king Cambyses I, but also grandson by his mother of the Median king Astyages, ascended the Persian throne. Immediately he attempted a political coup and overthrew the government, becoming sole ruler of the whole kingdom. The great political beast rolls over to its side, giving supremacy to the once inferior Persians. The book of Esther, in which the traditional expression "Medes and Persians" becomes "Persia and Media" (Esther 1:3), further confirms the rise of Persian supremacy.

Another characteristic of the beast is that it carries three ribs in its mouth. A similar passage in Amos mentions three pieces of flesh and bones recovered from the lion's mouth as the sole remains of his meal (Amos 3:12). It is another way to suggest the beast's voracity. The carnivorous character of the meal ("three ribs" or sides) echoes the bear's aggressive position ("on its side"). The passage then concludes: "Get up and eat your fill of flesh!"—a passage often understood as alluding to the three main conquests of the Persians: Lydia, Babylonia, and Egypt. But if these three conquests are but the remains, how much more did the conquering power of Cyrus actually devour! One college textbook declares:

"The Persian Empire had been created in a single generation by Cyrus the Great. In 559 B.C., he came to the throne of Persia, then a small kingdom well to the east of the lower Mesopotamian valley; unified Persia under his rule; made an alliance with Babylonia; and led a successful rebellion toward the north against the Medes, who were the overlords of Persia. . . . In succeeding years he expanded his empire in all directions, in the process defeating Croesus and occupying Lydia."[4]

The earliest sources of Jewish tradition already recognize, not without humor, the bear as representing the Persians: "Persians eat and drink like the bear, have hair like the bear, are agitated like the bear."[5] Another Talmudic passage calls the Persian guardian angel the "bear of Daniel."[6]

3. The Leopard

The leopard corresponds to the third kingdom of the statue and represents Greece. The addition of four wings intensifies the speed already characteristic of the leopard (Hab. 1:8). Likewise, the four heads multiplies the idea of domination. As we have already seen, the number four symbolizes totality and universality. This kingdom is, then, characterized by the rapidity and universality of its conquests: "And it was given authority to rule" (Dan. 7:6). The third kingdom is the only one to which dominion is specifically offered. Its predecessors never received such power as a gift. The lion gets "the heart of a man" (verse 4); the bear receives his "fill of flesh" (verse 5); but only the leopard has dominion ("authority to rule," verse 6) granted to it. Of course, each beast acquires a certain kind of dominion: the lion with a human heart receives the supremacy of humanity over beast, like Adam, whom God ordered to "rule over . . . every living creature" (Gen. 1:28; Jer. 27:5-7). The bear's dominion extends over the spatial and material world, but remains limited to a heap of "flesh." But for the leopard, the domination is complete. We go from "much" (literal translation of the Aramaic *sagî*, in the NIV "your fill") to "the whole earth" (Dan. 2:39). The leopard's domination encompasses much more than mere geographical conquest. It extends also on a cultural level. And indeed, Greek thought has infiltrated itself everywhere and constitutes the backbone of Western thought today.

Interestingly, dominion is not innate, but something granted by God. The verb "to give" (verses 4, 6) also renders the judgment of God (see chapter 1). The idea of God participating in the blood-soaked contortions of history can seem shocking. One should, however, not confuse the giving of power with its management. The power lies in God's hand. By giving it over to humans, He places the responsibility for it on them. The outcome is the person's sole doing, good or bad. It is another lesson of humility for the powerful, lest they imagine that the power they have sprouted from their own efforts. Scripture reminds us of its source and of our responsibility to handle it with care. And because God will one day reclaim the power, we are allowed to have hope. The God who started history will also finish it.

II. The Other Beast

In parallel to the fourth metal of the statue in chapter 2, this fourth beast represents Rome. As in chapter 2, its attributes are threefold: "terrifying and frightening and very powerful" (verse 7). Back in chapter 2 the iron metal was to "break," "smash," and "break things to pieces" (Dan. 2:40). Here in chapter 7 it "devours," "tramples," and "crushes" (Dan. 7:23). Significantly, this terrible beast has iron teeth (verse 7). Like the fourth kingdom of the statue, it differs from the other hybrids preceding it. The fourth kingdom of the statue was not all metal but was part clay. The beast distinguishes itself by having a horn with a human face (verse 8).

1. The Ten Horns

The 10 horns represent kingdoms emerging from the fourth kingdom symbolized by the beast (verse 24). As in the dream of the statue, the fourth kingdom ends up being divided.

History confirms this. In the last half of the fourth century the Germanic tribes would follow the initiative of the Huns and invade the then decadent Roman Empire, establishing upon its ruins "close to ten kingdoms."[7] The list of the kingdoms varies, but most historians would opt for "the Franks, the Burgundians, the Allaman [or Huns], the Vandals, the Suevi, the Visigoths, the Saxons, the Ostrogoths, the Lombards, and the Heruli."[8]

What the 10 kingdoms exactly represent is not really the issue. We must regard the number 10 in Daniel as symbolically alluding to a number beyond which it is impossible to count (cf. Gen. 18). The tenth also represents the smallest part (Isa. 6:13; Lev. 27:30), thus the kingdom could not be any more divided than it already is. In the statue dream of chapter 2 this period of division especially stands out, since it emerges from an era of unity and peace.

Actually, in the final analysis the kingdoms are of no relevance. The prophet is not interested in them, but rather in the bizarre little horn in their midst.

2. The Little Horn

This little horn with its human face (Dan. 7:20) greatly intrigues us. Actually, it presents the climax of the chapter and becomes Daniel's sole concern (verses 8, 24, 25). The little horn is the last and the greatest power, encompassing all that went before. The prophet portrays it in detail, enabling us to eventually recognize its face, the time of its coming, and the nature of its actions.

Its face. The human element of the little horn sets it apart from the other animal powers of the chapter. Likewise, the clay element of the fourth kingdom of the statue distinguished it from its metallic predecessors. In the biblical tradition human characteristics, as rendered by the human face and the potter's clay, have a religious connotation (see chapter 2 of our commentary). The little horn embodies, then, a political power, but with the reassuring features of the human face complete with mouth and eyes ever ready to testify to the religious aspect of things. We recognize here the fourth power of Daniel 2 with its dual political and religious nature.

Its time. The little horn appears chronologically after the 10 horns, causing in the process the downfall of three of them. History tells us that they originally belonged to the Arian branch of Christianity and were in perpetual conflict with the main body of the church, threatening its supremacy, especially since some of them (the Visigoths, the Vandals, and the Ostrogoths) had moved into Italy and neighboring regions. Catholic governors of the region considered it a sacred duty to eliminate their heretical influences. Clovis, king of the Franks (481-511), otherwise known as the "new Constantine," converted to Christianity (496? 506?). No sooner had he emerged from the baptismal waters than he took the offensive against the Visigoths of Vouille near Poitiers (508), decimating them. Justinian, governor of the eastern Roman Empire (527-565), declared the pope "ruler of all the holy priests of God"[9] and declared war on the Arians. Catholic forces crushed the Vandals in North Africa at the battle of Tricamarum in 534 and chased the Ostrogoths out of Rome in 538. The Italian peninsula was now free of Arian vestiges, and Catholic Christianity could now peacefully blossom on both religious and political levels.

The ratio of three out of 10 is also symbolic. In biblical arithmetic, the measure of three tenths appeared traditionally in the context of offerings (Lev. 14:10; Num. 15:9; 28:12, 20, 28; 29:3, etc.). Since the offering would be split up in three parts (Num. 15:6, 7; 28:14, etc.), the ration of three tenths would be rounded to one third so as to avoid complicated decimals. Three tenths would then be equivalent to one third. Biblical symbolic language employs the concept of one third to suggest the perspective of total destruction or total victory (Eze. 5:2; Zech. 13:8; Rev. 8:9; 9:18; 12:4). In other words, beyond the destruction of three kingdoms, the vision is alluding to the total destruction of all 10 kingdoms.

Its actions. The little horn directs its attacks on God and on His people. They are in fact interrelated, as suggested by the alternating parallelism describing them (Dan. 7:25):

A   He will speak against the Most High (against God)

B   and oppress His saints (against His people)

A_1 and try to change the set times and the laws (against God)

B_1 The saints will be handed over to him for a time, times, and half a time (against His people).

Against God. The little horn's first attack is a verbal one (verses 8, 20, 25): "This horn had . . . a mouth that spoke boastfully." The Aramaic term *rabreban* comes from the root *rab* (great, elevated) and conveys the idea of presumption and pride. The spirit of Babel has reincarnated itself into this emerging power whose goal is to usurp God.

But the arrogance of the little horn goes beyond words (A). It seeks as well to replace God on the level of history (A_1). In his first prayer (Dan. 2:21), Daniel refers to God as He who "changes times and seasons," an expression that he immediately explains: "He sets up kings and deposes them." The two clauses are related. Chapter 7 associates the same word for "time" with the possession of the kingdom: "the time came" (Dan. 7:22), implying the fact that God determines the time.

Against the people of God. Now the little horn turns against the "saints" in a surge of murderous revenge. By the way, they have nothing to do with halos and harps. In the book of Daniel the "saints" are those that belong to another kingdom (Dan. 4:17; 7:18, 22). Being foreigners, they are more vulnerable to persecution. In fact, as far as the book is concerned, "saints" is a synonym for "persecuted one" (Dan. 7:21; 8:24). Because they have their roots in the heavenly city of God, the "saints" pose a threat to the builders of the earthly "city of god" and shed doubt on their attempts to replace God Himself. Inquisitions, pogroms, and gas chambers are the deadly games of human beings playing God. Persecution is the fatal corollary of the human usurpation of God.

But the persecution of the saints does not remain an abstraction. Our text indicates its duration in time—it is to last "a time, times and half a time," that is, three years and a half. Our interpretation rests on several elements:

1. A preceding passage has used the same word for "time" *(idan)* in the sense of years (Dan. 4:16, 23, 25).

2. Aramaic understands the indefinite plural form "times" (Dan. 7:25) as a plural of duality (that is two times); thus adding up to a period of three years and half, that is 1260 days (the Jewish year, like the Babylonian year, follows the lunar calendar and consists of 360 days).

3. The same expression appears in Daniel 12:7 in relation to similar scopes of time (1290 days and 1335 days), all of which count down to the same time of the end (Dan. 12:7, 9, 11, 12).

4. The book of Revelation (Rev. 11:2, 3; 12:6; 13:5) further establishes our method of calculation. It uses the same formula, "one time, times and half a time," in relation to the event of persecution, converting it into 1260 days (Rev. 11:3 and 12:6) or into 42 months (Rev. 11:2; 13:5).

Thus situated in time, the period takes on a historical significance. Employing the information above, we can place it chronologically. There is, however, a contextual difference between the "times" of chapter 4 and the "times" of chapter 7. In chapter 4 the context was a historical one, while in chapter 7 we find ourselves in a prophetic context. The latter uses symbolic language that should not be taken literally. In the prophetic language of the Bible, one day symbolizes one year. Evidences for such usage appear in the book of Ezekiel, a prophet contemporary to Daniel and also in exile (Eze. 4:6). Traces of it are also present in the book of Daniel (see commentary on Daniel 9). We thus conclude that the expression "a time, times and half a time" signifies 1260 prophetic days, that is, 1260 years.

A study of prophetic chronology brings us to the year C.E. 538. Italy is completely rid of the Arians, especially of the Ostrogoths. The Christian church lays its foundations on what Y. Congar defines as the "basis of a hierarchico-descending vision, and finally a theocracy of power."[10] Gregory the Great (590-604) becomes, according to Jules Isaac, the "first pope to accumulate both political and religious functions."[11] From now on, the church has no more adversaries and is free to do as it pleases. The history of the medieval church leaves behind the bloody trail of the Crusades, of the Inquisition, of the massacres of Saint Bartholomew's Day, and of the Thirty Years' War. Thousands of victims—Protestants, Huguenots, Jews, even Catholics—preferred to shed their own blood rather than submit unthinkingly to the politico-religious institution. For a time, such oppression seemed justified. After all, as heretics, its victims were all bound for hell anyway. Yet, a few centuries earlier, the great Hillel had said that "even when the oppressor is right, God is always on the side of the victim." But the oppressor is never right. His violence is but the symptom of his own uncertainty, of his own failure. In any case, whatever the victims' identities, the righteous referred to by the prophet as the "saints" are always among them.

If the period of persecution begins in the year 538, it should end 1260 years later in 1798 (1260 plus 538). That year would see the Jesuit uprising, the rise of the Encyclopedists (philosophers of doubt), and the French Revolution with its outcry of rage against ecclesiastical authority. The French Revolution would confront the church with an atheistic society having but one god: reason.

But most important, in 1798 the French army under the commanding officer General Berthier would invade Rome, capture the pope, and deport him. General Bonaparte intended to eradicate papal and church authority. Ironically, it was France, the "eldest daughter of the Church," who had originally established the papacy as a political power. Now the nation would strip the pope of his prerogatives.[12]

Its identity. The little horn has become a political power under the guise of the church. In our ecumenical age such accusations seem unfair. After all, the Dark Ages are over, and so are the inquisitions and the crusades. The church of today works for world peace and sponsors humanitarian organizations. To bring up the prophecy would be out of place. And yet the present does not erase the past. The fact remains that the prophecy has been fulfilled. Even if the church does not persecute anymore, it still aspires for the divine pre-rogative to "set times" and "laws." Dogma has augmented biblical revelation, and Sunday, the first day of tradition, has replaced the seventh-day Sabbath of biblical revelation. That the church that God intended to witness for Him faces charges of usurpation naturally disturbs us. It greatly bothered Daniel himself. "I, Daniel, was deeply troubled by my thoughts, and my face turned pale" (Dan. 7:28; see also verse 15).

Our interpretation of the text is not new. Reformers such as Luther and Jewish authors such as Isaac Abarbanel had already antici-pated it. Generally, the Jews of the Islamic world saw in the little horn a power succeeding the Roman Empire, but representing Ishmael (Edom) rather than the church (as was the case for Saadia Gaon, Manasseh ben Israel, Ibn Ezra, etc.). Even Catholic authors such as the archbishop of Salzburg, Eberhard II (1200-1246), and the Portuguese Jesuit, Blasius Viegas (1554-1559) followed their line of interpretation, testifying, under an assumed name, against their own church.

In the heat of the argument, however, we must not rush into the extreme of seeing the features of the little horn on every aspect of Catholic Christianity. It is the Catholic Church as a historical and political institution that the prophecy denounces, not the believer as an individual. In fact, the evil represented by the little horn appears in any religious community that allows intolerance, anti-Semitism, and human tradition to prevail over love, respect, and faithfulness to divine revelation.

We must avoid misusing the prophetic message. Its principal objective is to throw new light on historical events and divine activity. Thus it is not an excuse for righteous anger. Likewise, to accept the better way of the prophecy does not necessarily mean that we must reject the old but must instead look for the fulfillment of a potential that had remained unnoticed or hidden. In spite of its political strategies and of its compromises, the church has nevertheless succeeded in reaching out to the world. Recognition of the truth of the prophecy should not lead us to anti-Catholicism.

On the other hand, we must accept truth with courage and honesty. Sincerity is not enough. It must be coupled with truth: "Sanctify them by the truth; your word is truth" (John 17:17). Fitness is not enough to win the race. We must also know in which direction to run. Respect and love go hand in hand with courage and honesty.

3. The Judgment

The verdict does not rest in our hands. All Christians are to some degree responsible and a part of the evil incarnated by the little horn. Under the same circumstances, many of us would have behaved in a truly "medieval" fashion, and would have participated with no less enthusiasm in the same policy of oppression and compromise. That is why the judgment is beyond human control. Scripture portrays it as an event situated in time and space, its verdict implicating the destiny of both the little horn and the saints.

The judgment described here undermines all our preconceptions about it. For example, we must not await it here and now in our present condition. The successes or misfortunes we encounter along the way are not the signs of divine judgment. During the Middle Ages such a belief led to the practice of ordeals in which presumed culprits endured fire or boiling water to prove their innocence. Society later abolished such barbaric practices in which innocence depended less on reason and equity than on luck or fraud.

Nor should we expect judgment even at death, the fatal moment that seals the direction of our soul. Neither is judgment to befall us at the resurrection.

For Daniel, the judgment is a unique and universal event taking place in the final moments of human history. The event of judgment appears in the last part of our text and coincides with the historical occurrence of the fourth beast and of the little horn. Judgment appears in the second part of the vision begun by the clause "After that, in my vision at night I looked" (Dan. 7:7) and by the "As I looked" that introduces the little horn (verse 9). The structure of the vision clearly situates the judgment before the end of human history. Verse 26 even seems to place it right after the 1260 years (hence after 1798): "The saints will be handed over to him for a time, times and half a time." The text then adds "but the court will sit" (verses 25, 26).

Daniel regards it as the most important event of the prophecy. Significantly, the chiastic structure of chapter 7 puts the judgment right at the center (see our structure of chapter 7). And since chapter 7 is at the middle of the book of Daniel, it follows that the judgment is at the center of the whole work of Daniel. Biblical tradition remembers the prophet in connection with divine judgment. The book of Ezekiel[13] (Eze. 14:14-20), the only other book in the Old Testament that refers to Daniel, associates the prophet with Job and Noah, two central figures of the theme of the judgment of God,[14] in a context of judgment (verses 13, 17-22). Likewise, in the New Testament, the only passage referring to Daniel deals with the great day of judgment (Matt. 24:15-21, 38, 39). Finally, Daniel himself testifies to the importance of divine judgment in the very name he bears: "Daniel" means precisely "judgment of God."

Judgment is the fulfillment of humanity's hopes and yearnings. In our minds it conveys the ideas of crime and punishment and inspires fear and apprehension. The Bible, however, sees judgment from the viewpoint of the oppressed, the suffering victim, and thus places it in the context of salvation and victory over the oppressor and evil. Israelite culture already recognized that fact on a national level. The judges of Israel were war heroes who would crush the enemy. Scripture also referred to them as saviors, *moshiah* (Judges 3:9, 15; 6:36; 12:3). This two-level aspect of the judgment of God is especially clear in the psalms that describe the judging God as both savior and avenger (Ps. 18:47, 48; 58:11; 94:1-6, 22, 23; 149:4, 7, 9; etc.). Such a depiction of God can shock our modern sensibilities.

And yet just coaxing the lion into letting go of the lamb will not work. To save the lamb, one must overcome the lion. That is why the term *tsedaqa,* which means "justice," implying the punishment of the oppressor, also means "love," as it liberates the oppressed back to life.

Chapter 7 of Daniel also explicates these two dimensions of divine judgment. The judgment is pronounced "in favor of the saints of the Most High" (verse 22) and against their enemies. In fact, the vision views judgment against a background of war and oppression: "As I watched, this horn was waging war against the saints and defeating them" (verse 21).

In the explanation of the vision (verses 26, 27), the judgment takes on two aspects: a negative one against the little horn that defeats and crushes him (verse 26), and a positive aspect for the saints who receive God's kingdom (verse 27). The scene of judgment is dominated by the images of "throne," "Ancient of Days," and "open books."

The throne is the first thing that Daniel notices. Right from the start the context defines the scene as a courtly one, testifying to the invisible presence of a king. But the throne is unlike other thrones. To describe it, Daniel uses the language of Ezekiel. In fact, it is the same throne! Both thrones give the impression of being aflame (Eze. 1:27; Dan. 7:9, 10) and both are mounted on wheels (Eze. 1:21; Dan. 7:9). The prophet Ezekiel describes the throne as having "the appearance of the likeness of the glory of the Lord" and then falls down in adoration (Eze. 1:28). Daniel is likewise awestruck, and uses the plural of emphasis "thrones." The equivalent in English would be "superthrone" (cf. Isa. 6:1). The rest of the passage clarifies the matter by having it seat no more than one person.

The vision of the throne clearly alludes to God's judgment. It evokes the seat of justice, and its fiery aspect is the biblical symbol of wrath, destruction, and judgment (Deut. 4:24; Ps. 18:9-14; 21:10; 50:3; 97:3). In the ancient Middle East, as a whole and in Israel in particular, judgment was a royal function. The king would make legal decisions while seated on his throne. This image of the king who judges is especially vivid in the psalms sung during the Temple services. The key expression "the Lord reigns" is usually linked to the notion of judgment.

Psalm 97, among others (Psalms 93; 99), begins with the phrase "The Lord reigns," continues with a description of God's throne founded on "righteousness and justice" before which fire "consumes his foes on every side" (verses 2, 3), and concludes with an explicit reference to God's judgment and royalty: "Because of your judgments, O Lord. For you, O Lord, are the Most High over all the earth; you are exalted far above all gods" (verses 8, 9).

The vision of the throne, as part of the scene of judgment, also reveals the divine kingdom. Monarchy is not our idea of perfection. The people do not elect God, and His government does not include different political parties. In fact, His presence dominates everything, and He has all control. Yet, such rulership was the greatest wish of the biblical heroes (Ps. 139:7-9; 33:5; 119:64; 104:24; Isa. 6:3; Num. 14:21; Hab. 3:3; Rom. 14:11; Phil. 2:10). All the enemies of God are wiped out. History is no longer adrift, no longer in the hands of fate or oppressors. The city of peace and of justice dreamed by the prophets did not have its origin in negotiations. Its walls ring with the shout of complete and radical victory over evil and death.

"The Ancient of Days" is a strange expression found nowhere else in the Bible, though similar expressions appear in Ugaritic (Canaanite) literature calling the great god El the "king, father of years" and judge.[15] The idea conveyed here is that of this king-judge's eternity, a concept reinforced by the imagery of white hair. Surrounded by multitudes of servants who attend Him, the Ancient of Days represents God Himself (cf. Ps. 68:18; Heb. 12:22). Moreover, He is the one who ascends the great throne to reign and to judge. In the biblical mind-set His old age best qualifies Him as judge. Age is a sign of wisdom. With a smile, the Talmud alludes to this passage in Daniel when it mentions God's hair as being black when He goes to war like a young man and white when seated in court like an old man.[16] The Ancient of Days was present at the beginning of time, as His name indicates. He knows every action when it is still unborn (Ps. 139:1-4). Only He knows the whole story and is in the best position to judge. His "clothing . . . as white as snow"

(Dan. 7:9) represents His character. He is a judge who cannot be bribed, and His verdict will be totally objective. Having had no part in the sin He is about to condemn, His moral faculties of judgment remain undulled. Only He knows good from evil, a paradox already enunciated in Genesis. When the man and woman sinned, evil mingled with good to the point that it became humanly impossible to separate them. The more people dedicate themselves to evil, the less they see it as such. Only He who never has been subject to evil can truly condemn it.

The books open immediately after the Ancient of Days takes His seat. It is the ultimate procedure of judgment. The prophet adds nothing more. The Bible generally depicts God as writing in a context of judgment (see chapter 5). The mention of books in the divine court also implies judgment. Their function is to record all past actions, and to serve as silent witnesses during the judgment (Ex. 13:9; 17:14). That is why the prophet Malachi speaks of a "scroll of remembrance" (Mal. 3:16-18). This perspective of remembrance again relates judgment to salvation.

For example, God remembers Noah (Gen. 8:1), Abraham, Isaac, Jacob (Ex. 32:13), Rachel (Gen. 30:22), Hannah (1 Sam. 1:19), and Israel (Ps. 115:12). In the psalms the victims of oppression cry out, "Remember, O Lord!" (Ps. 25:6; 74:2; 89:50; 119:49; etc.).

But God's remembrance can also bring about punishment. God remembers Amalek (1 Sam. 15:2), our iniquities (Ps. 79:8; Jer. 14:10), and Babylon (Rev. 16:19) and her iniquities (Rev. 18:5).

Likewise, "everyone whose name is found written in the book . . . will be delivered" (Dan. 12:1). Yet, it is also in the books that Daniel witnesses the execution of the little horn (Dan. 7:11, 12). The moment that the books open, however, does not coincide with the execution of the sentence. What Daniel sees in the books is only the verdict, whether guilty or not. The sentence comes later. Verses 11 and 12 announce the destiny of the little horn, more specifically of the fourth beast, carrier of the little horn. The destruction of the fourth beast is total, in contrast to the only partial destruction of the other three beasts, each one being the continuation of the former.

We should then read the verses announcing the death of the

fourth beast as anticipating a distant future while interpreting the verses describing the deaths of the other three beasts as a flashback to the past. Verses 10-12: "And the books were opened. Then I continued to watch [in the open books]. . . . I kept looking until the beast was slain and its body destroyed and thrown into the blazing fire. (The other beasts *had been* stripped of their authority, but *were* allowed to live for a period of time.)"

God intends the vision of judgment to be good news. In the twilight of human history the event of judgment is the last ray of hope. The judgment announces a new world, a new order, a city of peace and justice. The promise of the end of our misery, it predicts a new dawn.

III. A Son of Man

The last stage of the vision is the most fantastic and also the most disturbing. Riding upon the clouds, someone "like a son of man" (verse 13) rushes into view. His identity and his arrival on the scene greatly intrigue us.

1. His Identity

From the start the vision directly contrasts the son of man with that of the beasts, paralleling His "semblance" ("like a son of man") to the "semblance" of the beasts (like a lion, like an eagle, etc.). Also, the humanity of this "son of man" ("son of man" is the biblical idiom for someone of a human nature) sharply highlights the beastly attributes of the hybrids. The human is opposed to the animal. It is a contrast already hinted at in the beginning of the chapter through an allusion to the experience of Nebuchadnezzar (verse 4) and in preceding verses about the little horn (verse 8). In the language of Daniel, this contrast renders the essential difference between two fundamental orders: that of the beasts, and that of the "son of man." The animal symbolizes the political dimension of the earthly kingdoms while the human symbolizes the religious dimension of the kingdom of heaven, something already attested to by several passages (Dan. 2:45; 3:25; 4:34; 5:5, etc.).

In the context of the book of Daniel the "son of man" shares his essence with that of the kingdom of God. A Babylonian inscription

116

using the word *Barnash* (son of man) to designate a high dignitary of the kingdom, rather like the Spanish *Hidalgo,* helps us to understand this passage more clearly.[17]

Moreover, His coming upon the clouds clearly identifies Him with God, whose return Scripture describes in similar terms (Isa. 19:1; Ps. 18:10-13). The Jewish tradition is unanimous (Rashi, Ibn Ezra, Saadia Gaon, etc.) in recognizing such a personage as being the Messiah-King. The New Testament and later the Christian tradition have assimilated the concept "son of man" with Jesus Christ. It is from this passage that the early Christians derived their greeting of hope, *Maran atha,* "the Lord is coming." The Aramaic verb *atha* ("come") appears in our passage to describe the arrival of this "son of man" (Dan. 7:13).

2. His Coming

Daniel sees him "coming down" (verse 13, literal translation) from heaven. Hope arrives from elsewhere, a truth repeatedly emphasized throughout the Bible. Men and women cannot save themselves. They need God, who is external to them. Daniel describes the downward movement of the "son of man" through the use of seven verbs, the tenses of which render three distinct phases.

Phase 1 occurs during the contemporary period of the prophet and is presented by a verb in the participial tense: "And behold someone like a Son of man [was] *coming* on the clouds of heaven" (verse 13, literal translation).

During phase 2 the prophet looks in the past in relation to the participle above and pronounces three verbs in the Aramaic perfect tense, which we translate by a pluperfect: "He *had come* to the Ancient of Days, *had been brought* to him, and there *had been given* unto him the domination, the glory, and the kingdom" (verses 13, 14, literal translation).

Next, in phase 3 the prophet looks to the future in relation to the participle in phase 1 and utters three verbs in the Aramaic imperfect tense, which we translate by a future: "And all peoples, nations, and men of every language *will worship* him. His dominion is an everlasting dominion that *will* not pass away, and his kingdom is one that *will* never be destroyed" (verse 14).

In other words, between the coming of the Son of man, who in-

117

augurates the kingdom (phase 1), and the actual establishment of that kingdom (phase 3), the author inserts a flashback that sees the "son of man" in close encounter (*qrb,* verse 13) with the Ancient of Days on the occasion of judgment. Through these back-and-forth movements in time—present, past, future—the prophet indicates that one of the steps toward the establishment of the kingdom is a period of judgment. This same "son of man" who had participated in the procedure of judgment reappears to save the multitude of "saints" in the inauguration of His kingdom. The "son of man" has the last word on who will be saved and who will not. He is the link between the judgment and the kingdom. To pass from the judgment to the kingdom we must go through Him.

Our hope has not been vain. The prophet has spotted the "son of man" in the distant heavens. This link between heaven and earth, the one dreamed of by the patriarch Jacob as he slept on his stone (Gen. 28:11, 12), announced by the prophets, and longed for by the Psalms, the hope of Israel and of the Christians, is finally fulfilled. The whole structure of chapter 7 rests on this assumption. Three times the text alternates from prose to poetry, as the vision switches back and forth between heaven and earth.

verses 2–8	on the earth	in prose
verses 9, 10	in the heavens	in poetry
verses 11, 12	on the earth	in prose
verses 13, 14	in the heavens	in poetry
verses 15–22	on the earth	in prose
verses 23–27	in the heavens	in poetry

The sky and the earth seem to answer each other for the first time, as the sky is no longer empty. It finally has a voice—the voice of victory, of reconciliation. This is the heart of the book of Daniel. Chapter 7 is the chapter of hope, of renewed dialogue.

But in spite of this, Daniel is "deeply troubled." The events remain vague in time and in content. Daniel keeps the matter to himself (verse 28). He is still the prophet in exile waiting for redemption.

STRUCTURE OF DANIEL 7

Prologue: Visions of the head (verse 1)

A. Exposition of the vision (verses 2-14)

    I.   *The lion, the bear, and the leopard* (verses 2-6)

    II. *The other beast* (verses 7-12)

        a   The fourth beast

          b   The ten horns

            c   The little horn

> ### The Judgment

            c_1 The little horn

          b_1 The beast with ten horns

        a_1 The three beasts

    III. *The Son of Man* (verses 13, 14)

         ♦ Coming

         ♦ Flashback to judgment

         ♦ Kingdom of God

B. Explanations of the vision (verses 15-27)

    I.   *First explanation* (verses 15-18)

         ♦ The four beasts, the judgment, the kingdom

    II. *Request for further explanation* (verses 19-22)

         ♦ The fourth beast, the judgment, the kingdom

    III. *Final explanation* (verses 23-27)

         ♦ The fourth beast, the judgment, the kingdom

Epilogue: Trouble in thoughts (verse 28)

---

[1] Norman Porteous, *Daniel: A Commentary,* 2nd, rev. ed. (London: 1979), p. 95; see L. F. Hartman and A. A. Di Lella, *The Book of Daniel, Anchor Bible* (New York: 1977), vol. 23, p. 208.

[2] Lacocque, *The Book of Daniel,* p. 122.

[3] See the inscription of Nabonidus in Pritchard, *Ancient Near Eastern Texts,* pp. 562, 563.

[4] Donald Kagan, Steven Ozment, and Frank M. Turner, *The Western Heritage,* 3rd ed. (New York: 1987), p. 59.

[5] Babylonian Talmud *Kiddushin* 72a.

[6] Babylonian Talmud *Yoma* 77a.

[7] A. Alba, *Rome et le Moyen Age jusqu'en* 1328 (Paris: 1964), p. 164.

[8] See René Grousset and Emile G. Léonard, *Histoire Universelle,* vol. 1, Des origines à l'Islam, sous la direction de G. Grousset et E. G. Leonard (Paris: 1968), p. 349; cf. Charles

A. Robinson, Jr., *Ancient History: From Prehistoric Times to the Death of Justinian* (New York: 1951), pp. 658-665.

[9] P. DeLuz, *Histoire des Papes* (Paris: 1960), vol. 1, p. 62.

[10] *L'Eglise de St Augustin à l'époque moderne* (Paris: 1970), p. 32.

[11] *Genèse de l'Antisémitisme* (Paris: 1956), p. 196.

[12] The book of Revelation describes the same event. It sees the same 10-horned beast first wounded, then later completely healed (Rev. 13:3, 12). History shows that the papal authority, although shaken up by the eighteenth-century uprisings, was restored in the nineteenth-century Catholic revival (see Y. Congar, *L'Eglise de St. Augustin à l'époque moderne*, pp. 414, 415).

[13] The small difference in the spelling of the name of Daniel (in Ezekiel "Danel," without the *yod*) is not perceived as a valid argument against our identification. We know that the Massoretes added the *yod* much later, around the tenth century, as a vowel. Moreover, the Massoretic tradition suggests, in the margin of the text of Ezekiel 28:3, the alternative reading *(Qere)* "Daniel." This method of double reading is also attested for other names. For example, Genesis 46:24 calls the son of Naphtali Jahtseel and Jahtsiel (with a *yod*) in 1 Chronicles 7:13; likewise, the name of the Syrian king Hazael is written with the vowel-letter *hey* in 2 Kings 8:8 and without it in 2 Kings 8:9.

[14] The vision of Ezekiel 14 is dated in the sixth year of Jehoiachin (Eze. 8:1; 1:2), that is, 13 years after Daniel had arrived in Babylon, sign of the judgment of God against Israel (Daniel 1). Ezekiel was well acquainted with Daniel, and his allusion to him in the context of the judgment of God is not accidental. The progression of "Noah, Daniel and Job," mentioned twice in the passage (Eze. 14:14, 20), indicates the three levels of divine judgment, ranging from the general to the particular: the earth (Noah), the people of Israel (Daniel), the family and the individual (Job).

[15] See I AB 1.7; quoted in Lacocque, pp. 142, 143.

[16] Babylonian Talmud *Hagigah* 14a.

[17] A. Caquot, "Les quatres bêtes et le Fils d'Homme (Daniel 7)," in *Semitica* 17 (1967): 31-71.

THE KIPPUR WAR

We left chapter 7 with the prophet declaring, "I, Daniel, was deeply troubled." The beginning of chapter 8 echoes the "I, Daniel" (Dan. 8:1). Chapter 8 is the continuation of chapter 7. As we enter chapter 8 we find ourselves still concerned and troubled by the events of chapter 7. The relationship between the two visions is further implied by their chronological occurrences. The vision of chapter 7 takes place in the first year of the reign of Belshazzar; that of chapter 8 in the third year of the same reign (551 B.C.E.). This same pattern also appears in the introductions of chapters 1 and 2 (respectively the first and third years of the reign of Nebuchadnezzar) and in chapters 9 and 10 (the first and third years of the reign of Darius). The pattern links the two consecutive visions. Furthermore, the two visions have several common themes and cover the same historical time span until the end. Yet, the two visions remain fundamentally different. In form, we go from Aramaic back to Hebrew; and in content, the four beasts are now two very familiar animals fighting each other to death. It is a battle of Kippur, of atonement.

The struggle concludes with a strange ritual, the nature of which would preoccupy Daniel throughout the whole vision. But Daniel's trouble differs from the misfortune that befell the Israelis in 1973 during their Yom Kippur war. That which he sees (verses 3-12) and hears (verses 13, 14) goes far beyond the historical and geographical boundaries of Israel: the Kippur war of Daniel takes place on a cosmic scale.

I. What Daniel Sees

The vision has two parts, each introduced by the phrase "I looked up, and there" (verses 3, 5).

1. The Ram

As in chapter 7, the prophet spots the animal next to water. In chapter 7 it was the "great sea," the Mediterranean. Here, it is just a river next to the city of Susa, perhaps even a canal, as implied by the Hebrew term *ubal* (Dan. 8:2), which means "to conduct." Chapter 7 has the vision extending all around the Mediterranean. Here it does not go beyond the confines of the Persian Empire. As for the city of Susa, 230 miles east of Babylon, it would later become one of the wealthiest capitals of the Persian kings, their favorite residence, where they stored all their treasures. The presence of a canal already suggests prosperity. In the Babylonian world canals served as the basis for agricultural wealth and abundance. An inscription of Nebuchadnezzar refers to a Babylonian canal named *Libil-khigalla*, "May it bring abundance." The word *libil* ("which brings") derives from the same root as our word *ubal* (river, canal).[1]

On this background of wealth and prosperity Daniel spots a ram charging toward the west, the north, and the south—a colorful way to suggest the expanse of its conquests extending to three corners of the earth and omitting the corner of its origin, the east. Its voracious appetite for space, and its one horn higher than the other, remind us of the bear in chapter 7 with its craving for flesh and one side higher than the other. The ram thus represents the kingdom of the bear, that is, the kingdom of the Medes and Persians. The interpretation of the vision supports our conclusion (Dan. 8:20).

History confirms the prophecy. Four years later, in 547 B.C.E., Cyrus the Persian, having already conquered Media (see chapter 7), now overwhelms Lydia, extending the boundaries of his kingdom as far as the Aegean Sea. In 539 B.C.E. he finally takes over Babylon. The Persians, originally vassals of the Medes, overcame them and became, of the two horns, the longer one that "grew up later" (verse 3).

2. The Goat

The vision rolls on, and a goat bursts upon the scene and charges toward the ram, who remains standing beside the canal, as though to protect its access. Attacking the ram, the goat fatally wounds it. The vision emphasizes the goat's speed and its four horns, reminding us of the leopard in chapter 7, also defined by its speed and four heads (Dan. 7:6). The goat represents the Greeks, who come from the west, a conclusion further substantiated by the interpretation of the vision (Dan. 8:21).

History again confirms the prophecy. In 490 B.C.E. the Athenians defeated the Persians at the battle of Marathon. Later, the armies of Alexander plow through Arbela and crush the feeble Darius in 331 B.C.E., clearing the way to the golden cities of Babylon and Susa. Once conquered, their tremendous riches fall into the hands of Alexander. "Take that city [Susa], and then you need not fear to challenge Zeus for riches"[2] Aristogorus had declared to Cleomenes, king of Sparta, about Susa. And indeed, the newly acquired wealth of Alexander came to 50,000 talents, the equivalent of several million dollars. "The hereditary foe of Greece had been utterly defeated; . . . Alexander deliberately set fire to Xerxes' palace, in order that the world might clearly understand that one regime had given way to another."[3] Alexander takes the title "King of Persia." But ever more ambitious, he crosses over the high mountains of Asia and descends into the Hindus Valley. At the apex of his glory, at the age of 33 years, he succumbs to illness and dies, a victim of his own ambition. History fulfills the vision down to the smallest detail. "But at the height of his power his large horn was broken off." Four of Alexander's officers would divide his kingdom among themselves: "And in its place four prominent horns grew up toward the four winds of heaven" (verse 8).

3. The Little Horn

There appears then a new power whose appearance and activities remind us of the little horn in chapter 7.

1. As in chapter 7, a "little horn" represents it (verse 9).

2. As in chapter 7, it displays great arrogance (verse 23) and intelligence (verses 23, 25).

3. As in chapter 7, this power wants to usurp God. Like the Tower of Babel, the little horn "grew until it reached the host of the heavens" (verse 10). The link between the little horn and the Tower of Babel receives further confirmation by the use of the verb "to grow" *(gdl)*, repeated three times (verses 10, 11, 25) in our text. A word from the same root, the Bible uses it to characterize the Tower of Babel *(migdal)*. The attempt to usurp God takes place on two levels.

First, like the little horn in chapter 7, the one in chapter 8 assumes the prerogatives of the "Prince of the host" (verse 11) and takes the "daily sacrifice" (literally "perpetual sacrifice") from Him. This sacrifice burned permanently on the altar *(tamid:* "perpetual") and symbolized God's faithful presence among His people. "This burnt offering is to be made regularly. . . . There I will meet you and speak to you. . . . Then I will dwell among the Israelites and be their God. They will know that I am the Lord their God, who brought them out of Egypt so that I might dwell among them" (Ex. 29:42-46). In seizing the "daily sacrifice," the horn substitutes itself for God in the religious experience.

Furthermore, like the little horn of chapter 7, the one in chapter 8 despises the law: "Truth was thrown to the ground" (literally "trampled," verse 12). The word *emeth* rendered here by "truth" is synonymous with "law" (see Ps. 43:3; 119:43, etc.). In Hebrew, truth is a concrete action of obedience to God and has nothing to do with our abstract conception of truth. It is anything in accordance with the law. The word *emeth* derives from the root *aman* (the source of our expression "Amen"), which means "to obey," "to be faithful," and implies a reference to a higher authority. Jewish commentators (Ibn Ezra, Rashi) interpreted the verse to mean that "the little horn shall annul the Law [Torah] and the observance of the commandments."[4]

4. As in chapter 7, this power also persecutes the saints (verse 24).

5. And finally, as in chapter 7, the little horn succeeds the reign of beasts and remains to the end the sole power. Undoubtedly, it is the same as the one encountered in chapter 7.

The only difference would be its origin. Unlike the little horn of chapter 7, which emerged from one of the four beasts, the little horn of chapter 8 arises from one of the four winds of heaven (Dan. 8:8). This expression brings us back to the origins of the four beasts in chapter 7: the sea churned up by the four winds of heaven (Dan. 7:2). The little horn would, then, have emerged from one of those winds and not from one of the horns, as some translations seem to imply. First of all, normally the horn grows from the head and not from another horn. Furthermore, in the book of Daniel, when a horn appears after previous ones, it is always at the price of the downfall of some of them (Dan. 7:8; 8:8).

Grammatically speaking, the Hebrew expression translated as "out of one of them" (Dan. 8:9) we should actually read as "out of one [feminine] of them [masculine]," suggesting a link with the preceding expression: "the four winds [feminine] of heaven [masculine]." In Hebrew poetry, this is known as a grammatical parallelism with the alliterations of *t* and *m:*

Winds (F) of heaven (M): *ruhot hashamaim*

Out of one (F) of them (M): *ahat mehem* (verses 8, 9)

Through the use of the four winds Daniel alludes to the four beasts. In mentioning that the horn comes from one of the winds, he is implying that it originates in one of the beasts. The prophet purposely makes no mention of the beasts to keep the attention of his readers solely on the ram and on the goat.

4. The Association of the Ram and Goat

The question remains as to why the vision of chapter 8 replaces the cycle of four animals with only two animals, and the most insignificant at that. It omits the first and fourth kingdoms, both considered primary by Daniel: Babylon, the present residence of Daniel represented by the "head" and the "lion" (Dan. 2:37, 38; 7:4) and Rome, the strange kingdom that would profoundly disturb Daniel (Dan. 2:40; 7:7, 19). And why this sudden retreat from the fantastic to the familiar, from the bizarre hybrid beasts representing pagan kingdoms, to two ordinary animals classified as clean by Levitical laws?

If Daniel has decided to use the two middle kingdoms as the main characters of his vision, it is precisely because of their insignificance. His main focus is actually not the kingdoms themselves but the two animals: the ram and the goat.

Their association becomes significant in the context of the greatest Jewish yearly festival, Yom Kippur, the Day of Atonement (Lev. 16:5). Yom Kippur had as its traditional sacrifice the dual offering of a ram and a goat. Beyond their representations of the Medo-Persian and Greek kingdoms, the two animals also evoked the Day of Atonement.

The Levitical atmosphere defines itself even more in the actions of the little horn, which involve the "daily sacrifice," "sin," and the "sanctuary" (Dan. 8:11, 12). The passage even mentions the highest officiant of the sacrificial system, the high priest. The Hebrew word translated as "Prince" or "chief" (*sar;* verses 11, 25) is the technical term for high priest (Ezra 8:24). In the context of the book of Daniel the word refers to Michael (Dan. 10:5, 13, 21; 12:1) who is dressed with linen clothes like the high priest officiating during the Day of Kippur (Lev. 16:4).

But the next scene is even more explicit in its references to the Day of Kippur.

II. What Daniel Hears
1. A Judgment

In those tragic moments of victory for the little horn, the vision goes from sights to sounds. Daniel overhears a conversation between two divine beings. The same thing happened in the vision of chapter 4, where also sound replaced sight, and Daniel heard the voice of a being, also referred to as "a holy one" (Dan. 4:13, 14, 23; 8:13). In using the same wording as in chapter 4, Daniel suggests a similar context of judgment. This time a question shouted by one of the saints precipitates the decision: "Until when this vision of the perpetual: the devastating sin delivered, and the sanctuary and the army trampled?" (Dan. 8:13, literal translation).

Almost all the words cited by this verse allude to the preceding actions of the little horn: "vision" (verse 1); "perpetual" (verses 11, 12); "delivered" (verse 12); "sanctuary" (verse 11); "army" (verses 10-12); "trampled" (verse 10). The passage speaks against its behavior. The reference to the perpetual offering and all related subjects (sin, deliver, sanctuary, law, etc.) protests the little horn's attempt to replace God and thus surround itself with religious terminology. The mention of the army and related subjects (surrender, trample) points to the persecution of the saints. "How long will [all this] take?" "How long?" *(ad matay?)*. In the psalms the expression was the cry of the oppressed (Ps. 6:4; 13:2; 62:3; 74:10; 94:3, etc.). And to their cry comes the shout of hope.

The same word that formulates the question—*"ad"* (until)—introduces the answer given by a second saint.

"Until when?" questions one saint (see Dan. 8:13).

"Until 2300 evenings and mornings; then the sanctuary will be cleansed," replied another (see verse 14).

Only after 2300 evenings and mornings will the destructive rampage of the little horn stop, an interpretation later offered by the angel Gabriel: "Yet he will be destroyed, but not by human power" (verse 25). The end of the little horn will not result from natural causes, but from an extraordinary act of judgment on God's part, closing the circle of history (Dan. 2:34; 11:45).

As in chapter 7, the behavior of the little horn is judged from above and later destroyed (Dan. 7:10-12). Chapter 8 follows the same structure as chapter 7:

Chapter 7: beasts/kingdoms—little horn—judgment

Chapter 8: beasts/kingdoms—little horn—cleansing of the sanctuary

According to the parallelism between the two chapters, the event described in chapter 8 as the cleansing (or reconsecration) of the sanctuary would then correspond to the day of judgment in chapter 7. Significantly, the Septuagint translates this term with the Greek word *katharisai* (to purify), a technical word used to refer to Kippur.[5] The great Jewish commentator Rashi also suggests that we should read this passage in the context of the Day of Atonement.[6]

What chapter 7 calls the Day of Judgment chapter 8 labels as the Day of Atonement. They are in fact the same event. Israel experienced the Day of Atonement as the actualization of the last judgment.

Leviticus 16 introduces the ceremony of Kippur by an allusion to the judgment. The text begins with the death of Aaron's sons, struck by divine fire, and with the threat of death that remains as a shadow over the rest of Israel (verses 1, 2), extending over the totality of the people (verses 33, 34). The ritual itself is rich in connotations of judgment: the separation of the two goats, one pure, the other impure; the fate *(goral)* that separates them (verses 8-10); the obligation to fast and to humiliate one's soul (verse 29); the multiple blood aspersions (verses 15, 19, 27); and the ablutions (verses 24, 26, 30, etc.).

Even today the Jews celebrate Kippur as a day of judgment or of atonement. During the whole year one may forget God and religion and commit crimes. But even the greatest villain, if he is Jewish, will repent on the Day of Atonement and tremble at the sound of the shofar, the sign of divine judgment. Jews identify Kippur with the day of judgment. The prayers recited on that day are significant:

"We must give all holiness to this day, for it is a day of fear and trembling. On this day, your reign shall be established and your throne affirmed. . . . For you are the judge, the prosecutor, and the witness, he who writes and seals. And you will remember the things long-forgotten, and open the book of memory. . . . Then shall sound the great shofar, and the voice of silence shall be heard, the angels shall be gripped by fear and trembling and shall say: 'Behold, the day of Judgment!'" [7]

According to an old tradition, on the day of Kippur "God, seated on His throne to judge the world, at the same time Judge, Pleader, Expert, and Witness, openeth the Book of Records; it is read, every man's signature being found therein. The great trumpet is sounded; a still, small voice is heard; the angels shudder, saying, this is the day of judgment." [8]

In fact, the Jewish tradition has the judgment of Kippur start from the first day of the month, hence of the year (Rosh Hashanah). The two festivals have had a long association. Each enacts the same ritual (Num. 29:1-5, 8-11) and one hears the same sounds of the shofar (Lev. 25:9; 23:24). [9]

Jews have understood the 10 days preceding Kippur as a probationary time during which they prepared for the day of judgment. The traditional greeting during that period is *Hatima tova,* "May you be well sealed"—an allusion to the divine judgment that will decide each individual's destiny and seal it.

"To the average individual, who is neither totally corrupted nor

totally good, shall be accorded ten days [Tishri 1 to Tishri 10]; they have until Kippur to repent, in which case they shall live; otherwise death will punish their sinful behavior." [10]

2. A Creation

According to Leviticus 16, this festival had cosmic implications. The people submitted "all the iniquities of the people" to divine judgment. The expression "all their sins" runs as a leitmotiv in Leviticus 16 (verses 21, 22, 30) and also appears in the psalm inspired by this great festival (Ps. 130:8). The Day of Atonement is the moment where the sins of *all* Israel receive atonement, or forgiveness. Forgiveness was ensured during the year through the "perpetual" sacrifice, but on the Day of Atonement, it needed the backup of other sacrifices. The expiation of sin was not an individual matter anymore. The Day of Atonement was the only time when the totality of the people of Israel and the whole space of the sanctuary were totally "purified" (Lev. 16:17, 33, 34). It was also the only time that the high priest could enter the Holy of Holies in the sanctuary and physically present himself to God (Ex. 30:6-10; Lev. 16:2, 14). And the only time when the Great Pardon of God extended beyond the simple, individual pardon. Sin was not only forgiven, but banished from the camp. The high priest chased "Azazel," the incarnation of sin, into the desert (verse 21).

But this ceremony enacts more than the judgment. The cleansing of the sanctuary is in fact the sign of the total purification of the whole earth on the day of God's judgment. Biblical theology understood the Israelite sanctuary as representative of the whole world that God created. The description of the construction of the sanctuary in Exodus 25-40 parallels the narration of the creation of the world in Genesis 1:1-2:4. Both occur in seven stages and both end with the same technical phrase: "finished the work" (Gen. 2:2; Ex. 40:33). The construction of the Temple by Solomon also takes place in seven stages and ends with the same words: "finished the work" (1 Kings 7:40, 51). The phrase appears only in these three passages of the Bible and clearly indicates the relationship between the sanctuary-temple and Creation. The psalms also attest to that connection: "He built the sanctuary like the high mountains, like the earth that he established forever" (see Ps. 78:69; cf. 134:3; 150:1, 6).

In a way, Kippur reminds us, then, of the weekly Sabbath, evoking like that day the creation of the world (Ex. 20:11; cf. Gen. 2:1-3). Significantly, of all the festivals depicted in the book of Leviticus we find the book setting only these two, the Sabbath and the Day of Atonement, apart as a day when the people are to "do *no* work," as opposed to doing "no regular work" (Lev. 23:3, 28, 35, etc.).

For the Israelite, Kippur symbolized the purification of the world, a true re-creation. This is why Daniel uses the expression "evenings and mornings" (Dan. 8:14), a phrase that occurs strictly in the context of Creation (Gen. 1:5, 8, 13, 19, 23, 31).

Jewish tradition also associated the idea of Creation, like that of judgment, with the day of Kippur. The ancient Midrash, interpreting the first verses of Creation, declares: "There was an evening, and there was a morning, one day, this means that the Holy One, Blessed be He, gave them (Israel) one day, which is none other than the day of Kippur."[11]

The prayers recited on Yom Kippur remind the believer that the God who judges is also the Creator who forgives. "Blessed art thou, O Lord our God, King of the Universe, who opens the doors of Your grace and opens the eyes of those who wait for the forgiveness of Him who has created light and darkness, and all things."[12]

"How is the human to be just before his Creator, when he stands naked before Him?"[13]

The prophecy of Daniel sees on the horizon of history a heavenly Kippur described in terms of judgment and creation. The Kippur the Israelites celebrated in the desert is but a rough draft of the heavenly Kippur. The two events belong to two totally different orders. And yet, to comprehend the divine Kippur, one must understand the earthly Kippur. Its spiritual message reminds us that history will come to an end, that the God-Judge will rise to seal the destiny of the human race and prepare for them a new kingdom.

We understand now the relevance of both judgment and of creation during such moments in history. In fact, judgment and creation operate the same way. Judgment elects a new people, torn from the grip of sin and suffering, a people set apart, separated from the others, but also a forgiven people. Creation fashions a new world, released from the shadow of death, a purified planet. In this context, judgment is synonymous with creation, as both imply a radical separation.[14] Kippur is simultaneously the awareness of divine judgment and the hope of re-creation.

On the one hand, the awareness of the judgment of God invites us to repentance. Yom Kippur was the day for the Israelite to "deny himself" (Lev. 16:29, 31), the day to assume responsibility for one's actions. God "created [the] inmost being" and weighs all actions (Ps. 139). But believing in divine judgment does not imply the mournful attitude of someone groveling in misery and sinfulness, permanently undergoing judgment. On the contrary, "be happy, . . . let your heart give you joy in the days of your youth. Follow the ways of your heart and whatever your eyes see, but know that for all these things God will bring you to judgment" (Eccl. 11:9). Judgment does not exclude the enjoyment of life—rather it implies it. Our awareness of judgment provides the frame in which we can best experience life.

The promise of re-creation also validates our hope. We can expect real change. True salvation is historical, not just spiritual. We cannot save ourselves in our present condition. Only God can, and to do so He must transform the world—the essential meaning behind the festival of Kippur. An old story tells of 10 rabbis, righteous and just, tortured to death by the Romans. The prayer book narrates that a voice then tore through the heavens and cried: "Is this then the reward of the just?" to which God answered: "Shut up! or I destroy the world!" No other solution exists to the problem of evil. Salvation implies the destruction of the very cause of suffering and death. Not a mystical or psychological experience, salvation is an event of cosmic proportions that comes from beyond and is situated in history.

We remember that chapter 7 located the judgment "after a time, times and half a time," that is, after 1798. Chapter 8 is even more explicit: the reign of the little horn lasts 2300 evenings and mornings. The expression "evening-morning," borrowed from the story of Creation, represents a day that we should understand in the prophetic sense as a year (equaling 2300 years). But this new information is not much help. A period of time with no indication of its starting point could be suspended anywhere in history. The angel Gabriel merely specifies that it leads to the end: "Understand that the vision concerns the time of the end" (verse 17; also see verse 26).

Daniel is "appalled by the vision" that he finds to be "beyond understanding" (*eyn mebin,* verse 27). We leave chapter 8 on a note of frustration because we need more information to understand its vision. But the comprehension we must have is not of a philosophical order. Our intelligence does not stumble here on the complexity of an abstract truth, but on the time of the predicted event. The prophet understands that it involves a question of the end of time. The book of Daniel employs the same word, "understand" *(bin),* for the prophecy of the 70 years (Dan. 9:22) and later for the prophecy of the 70 weeks.[15] What he doesn't understand is exactly when in the end of time. The focus is less on the theological implications of the prophecy than on an event that will take place at a given moment.

Until it receives a starting date, the prophecy remains an abstraction and subject to doubt. To become the object of hope, the promise of re-creation must be inserted in the chronology of history.

Judgment and re-creation are the two faces of Kippur. It is not surprising that the book of Revelation mentions them as the two vectors of faith during the last days. Entering in the cycle of Daniel 7, right before the coming of the Son of man—that is, during the celestial Kippur—the prophecies of Revelation 13 and 14 mention a messenger bearing precisely the dual message of judgment and creation: "He said in a loud voice, 'Fear God and give him glory, because the hour of his judgment has come. Worship him who made the heavens, the earth, the sea and the springs of water'" (Rev. 14:7).

According to the book of Revelation, which arises out of the book of Daniel, the last days will resound with new adoration embracing both notions of judgment and creation. This adoration will be more than an emotional or a spiritual experience. It will spring from the hope in the divine judgment and salvation and the faith in creation. Even more, this adoration will testify to the very faith of the Bible, the book that begins, indeed, with creation (Gen. 1; Matt.

1; John 1) and ends with judgment and salvation (Mal. 4:2; 2 Chron. 36:21-23; Rev. 22:17-21).

STRUCTURE OF DANIEL 8

Introduction: "I Daniel"; reference to the king

I. **Vision**

What he sees (verses 3-12):

1. "I saw . . . and behold"
   - the ram (verses 23, 24)
2. "I saw . . . and behold"
   - the goat with one horn (verses 5-8)
   - the four horns (verse 8b)
   - little horn (verses 9-12)

What he hears (verses 13, 14):

"Kippur" (verses 13, 14)

II. **Interpretation of the Vision**

1. What he sees: appearance of a man (verse 15)
2. What he hears:
   - Make understand the vision (verses 16-19)
   - Ram: Medes and Persians (verse 20)
   - Goat: *Yavan* (verse 21)
   - Four horns: four kingdoms (verse 22)
   - At the end:
     - rise of a power (verses 24, 25a)
     - success (verses 24, 25a)
     - fall (verse 25b)
   - Vision of the evenings and mornings (verse 26)

Conclusion: "I Daniel"; reference to the king; stay without understanding (verse 27)

---

[1] Cf. Charles Boutflower, *In and Around the Book of Daniel* (London: 1923), p. 217.

[2] Herodotus 5. 49.

[3] Robinson, p. 336.

[4] *Miqraoth Gdoloth.*

[5] See Leviticus 16:30 in the Septuagint Bible.

[6] *Miqraoth Gdoloth.*

[7] Author's translation from Prayer Book, *Mahzor minroch hachana weyom hakippurim,* first part, 31.

[8] "Atonement, Day of," *The Jewish Encyclopedia* (1902).

[9] See *Entsiklopedia Miqraoth* 3 (1965), 595; cf. K. Hrubi, "Le Yom ha-Kippurim ou Jour de l'Expiation," *Old Testament Studies* 10 (1965): 58ff. Note also that the Beney Israel celebrate both festivals as one (Van Goudoever, *Fêtes et calendriers bibliques* (1967), p. 57ff.

[10] Babylonian Talmud, *Rosh Hashana,* 16b.

[11] Midrash Rabbah, *Genesis* 4. 10.

[12] *Yotser leyom Kippur.*

[13] *Mosaph leyom Kippur.*

[14] Gordon J. Wenham, *Genesis 1-15, Word Biblical Commentary,* vol. 1 (Waco, Tex.: Word, 1987), p. 18.

[15] See also Dan. 12:7, 8, which links the verb "understand" to the period "a time, times and half a time" and "the time of the end" (verses 9, 11).

CHAPTER 9

REQUIEM FOR A MESSIAH

I. The Messiah of 70 Years

The last words of chapter 8 still resound in our ears as Daniel finds himself left in total darkness, "beyond understanding" (Dan. 8:27). He had to wait 13 years to receive light on the subject. We are now in the first year of the reign of Darius (538 B.C.E.), a year stamped with the seal of hope. It is the same year of Daniel's encounter with the lions, of his rescue by the angel (Dan. 6). Beyond that, it witnesses the first prophecies fulfilled (chapters 2 and 7): Babylon surrenders to the Medes and Persians. Finally, it is the year of the reign of Cyrus, whose coregent is Darius in Babylon. The prophet Isaiah had appraised Cyrus as a messiah and savior of Israel: "He is my shepherd and will accomplish all that I please; he will say of Jerusalem, 'Let it be rebuilt,' and of the temple, 'Let its foundations be laid.' This is what the Lord says to his anointed, to Cyrus, whose right hand I take hold of . . . : 'I will go before you and will level the mountains. I will give you . . . riches . . . so that you may know that I am the Lord, the God of Israel, who calls you by name. For the sake of Jacob my servant, of Israel my chosen, I call you by name and bestow on you a title of honor, though you do not acknowledge me'" (Isa. 44:28-45:4).

As Daniel observes the fulfillment, he begins to understand and wants to know more. The last negative "understanding" of the previous chapter (Dan. 8:27) now has a positive "understood" in Daniel

9:2: "I, Daniel, understood from the Scriptures, according to the word of the Lord given to Jeremiah the prophet, that the desolation of Jerusalem would last seventy years."

The preceding vision had a disappointing aftertaste. For an instant Daniel could have jumped to the conclusion that the devastation of Jerusalem was to last 2,300 years. But after consulting the book of Jeremiah, he finds himself reassured. The exile would not exceed 70 years. "This is what the Lord says: 'When seventy years are completed for Babylon, I will come to you and fulfill my gracious promise to bring you back to this place. . . . Then you will call upon me and come and pray to me, and I will listen to you'" (Jer. 29:10-12; cf. 25:11, 12).

In the conclusion of the Hebrew Bible, the book of Chronicles reformulates the prophecy of Jeremiah, making this time a direct reference to Cyrus. As for the period of 70 years itself, the passage views it as a reference to the Sabbatical year (7 x 10):

"He [Nebuchadnezzar] carried to Babylon all the articles from the temple of God. . . . He carried into exile to Babylon the remnant, who escaped from the sword, and they became servants to him and his sons until the kingdom of Persia came to power. The land enjoyed its sabbath rests; all the time of its desolation it rested *[shabbat]*, until the seventy years were completed in fulfillment of the word of the Lord spoken by Jeremiah. In the first year of Cyrus king of Persia, in order to fulfill the word of the Lord spoken by Jeremiah, the Lord moved the heart of Cyrus king of Persia to make a proclamation throughout his realm and to put it in writing: 'This is what Cyrus king of Persia says: "The Lord, the God of heaven, . . . has appointed me to build a temple for him at Jerusalem in Judah. Anyone of his people among you—may the Lord his God be with him, and let him go up"'" (2 Chron. 36:18-23).

So of the 70 years, beginning in 605 B.C.E. with the destruction of Jerusalem (Dan. 1), 68 years had gone by and still nothing happened. The people are still in exile and Jerusalem in ruins. Strengthened by his own experience with prophecy, Daniel grapples with this last promise. He develops a renewed interest in prophecy through the events of the past year. Having witnessed its partial fulfillment, he longs for more.

Sensing the 70 weeks slowly drifting by without any sign of change, Daniel throws himself at God's feet in prayer.

II. An Impatient Prayer

The prophet utters his prayer in great anguish and from behind the mask of death. The text mentions three symbols of death: Fasting, sackcloth, and ashes (Dan. 9:3). Such a ritual of repentance often accompanied prayer in biblical times. Like the dead, one does not eat and wears only the most rudimentary clothes—a rough garment of ram's wool or camel hair. Also like the dead, one crumbles back to ashes. The Israelite assumes the appearance of death when praying, for before God one is as naked and vulnerable as in death. As dust the person calls upon his Creator, the source of his life. In his prayer Daniel concentrates his whole being. Becoming the prayer, he feels that nothing else matters but what he implores. The longest and most important prayer in the book of Daniel, *it is the seventh and last prayer*.

For the first time the prayer is truly universal, as it involves all the people of Israel. Its "chiastic" structure (A B C B$_1$ A$_1$) already implies this universality, climaxing in C, its geometrical center:

A	verse 4	invocation of the Lord
B	verses 5, 6	we have been wicked
C	verses 7, 8	"all Israel"
B$_1$	verses 10, 11	we have not obeyed
A$_1$	verses 15-19	invocation of the Lord

The sin of Israel overflows into the neighboring lands: "Our sins and the iniquities of our fathers have made Jerusalem and your people an object of scorn to all those around us" (verse 16). Likewise, the catastrophe that befell the people and the city of Jerusalem has cosmic proportions: "Under the whole heaven nothing has ever been done like what has been done to Jerusalem" (verse 12).

For the first time Daniel prays in the first-person plural: "We have sinned and done wrong" (verse 5); "We have not listened to your servants the prophets" (verse 6); "Our sins and the iniquities of our fathers" (verse 16). But the "we" of the people interweaves with the "you" of God.

The first part of the prayer contrasts the "we" subject of the rebellion (verses 5, 6:B) with the "you" subject of God's faithfulness (verse 4:A). Likewise, in the second part, the "we" subject of the people's rebellion (verses 10-14:B₁) stands juxtaposed with the "you" subject of the grace of God (verses 15-19:A₁). The two parts answer to each other following a chiastic structure A B // B₁ A₁.

But it is in the heart of the prayer (verses 7-9) that we find the two elements most tightly bound, also in a chiastic structure a b c b₁ a₁.

a   to you (verse 7)
b   we are covered with shame (verse 7)
c   all Israel (verse 7)
b₁   we are covered with shame (verse 8)
a₁   to you (verse 9)

Such an alternating structure suggests the dynamics of responsorial chanting in Israelite liturgy. The style of Daniel's prayer reminds the reader of the psalms (Ps. 46; 47; 75; 106; 115; 137, etc.) and of the prayers of Ezra (Ezra 9:6-15) and Nehemiah (Neh. 1:5-11; 9:5-38) of which Daniel echoes several themes. The religious assembly could easily chant the prophet's prayer in a context of adoration. It is not a prayer confined to Daniel's upper room (chapter 6), but one that involves the destiny of all Israel. Not just a personal exercise, religion also has a social and cosmic dimension that transcends the individual. Hence the liturgical exercise. Saints who withdraw so as to better criticize their neighbors end up creating an idolatrous religion in their own image. But Daniel escapes this temptation and includes himself with the people of Israel. He does not triumph from a pedestal far above the filth of the people. As intercessor for Israel before God, Daniel embodies their sins himself. His intercession for them is passionate, as he is himself implicated in the destiny of his people. And Daniel endures exile also as a result of the sin of his fathers (Dan. 9:12, 13). The liturgical "we" encompasses both past and future generations. The God of Daniel is also the God of the Exodus who brought Israel out of Egypt (verse 15). The name *YHWH,* the name of the God of history, the God of covenant, never before mentioned in the book of Daniel, now appears sevenfold (verses 4, 9, 10, 13, 14, 20). *YHWH* is also the God of the future in that He is to save Israel from exile. The prayer of Daniel roots the "we" not only in the iniquities of the past generations, but also in their experiences of salvation. And this is what nourished the prophet's hope.

The liturgical experience is a beautiful and moving one. The prayer is profound and finds an echo within our souls. Uplifted by the voices that surround us, we feel a sense of belonging, of harmony. But such an experience is true only when inserted in the flow of history. The liturgical experience in the Bible always involves a remembrance of past events and a hope for future ones. Liturgy always plunges its roots deep in real existence.

Daniel is praying for his people and for the city of Jerusalem in ruins (verse 19). As in chapter 6, he prays in the direction of Jerusalem and its destroyed Temple: "making my request to the Lord my God for his holy hill" (verse 20).

The moment his prayer takes place is also significant: "about the time of the evening sacrifice" (verse 21). It is the time not only for Daniel to break his fast (Ezra 9:5), but also for the events he prayed for to be fulfilled (Ps. 141:2; 1 Kings 18:36).

Even in a liturgical context, the prayer must have historical repercussions. Without the reference to history, prayer is only a hollow rite, a fleeting emotion.

The transition from the human outcry to history occurs at the conclusion of the prayer with the technical phrase "and now" (Dan. 9:4, 17). We are back to the first person, as in the introduction of the chapter (verses 3, 4). But the transition from the human outcry to the divine answer does not result from the rite, but through the grace of God, already suggested by the "we-you" movement of the prayer; especially in the conclusion. The accumulation of divine pronouns is particularly suggestive: "in keeping with all your righteous acts" (verse 16), "because of your great mercy" (verse 18), "for your sake, O my God" (verses 17, 19). In fact, Daniel does not even need to finish praying for God to answer him. The angel visits him as he is still praying (verses 20, 21). The prayer has no value by itself. Words, no matter how true and beautiful, have no magical power to force God into action. God alone decides, and He alone acts. It all depends on Him.

That is why Daniel's prayer is so intense, so urgent: "O my God, do not delay" (verse 19). More than an immediate spiritual relationship, he wants change—historical, concrete change. His prayer focuses on the future entirely.

III. The Messiah of the 70 Weeks

God's answer to the prayer of Daniel and to his question concerning the 2300 evenings and mornings is Gabriel's announcement of the Messiah: "Know and understand this: From the issuing of the decree to restore and rebuild Jerusalem until the Anointed One, the ruler, comes, there will be seven 'sevens,' and sixty-two 'sevens'" (Dan. 9:25).

Biblical tradition regards the Messiah as a person set apart with a divine mission to save God's people. The Hebrew word *mashiah* (messiah) is a passive form of the verb *mashah* (to anoint). *Mashiah* (Messiah) designates the individual "anointed." The person designated as a messiah usually went through a ceremony that initiated his role. Someone anointed the person with oil, symbolizing the transmission of strength and wisdom as well as the faith of the anointer in the success of the newly appointed messiah.

Priests, prophets, and even kings were anointed to become messiahs. The history of Israel records several messiahs. Scripture calls Aaron a messiah (Ex. 28:41; Lev. 16:32), likewise the prophet Isaiah (Isa. 61:1), Saul (2 Sam. 1:14), David (1 Sam. 16:6, 13), and even a foreign prince, Cyrus (Isa. 45:1). The hope of Israel thus maintained itself from messiah to messiah.

The prophecy of the 70 weeks comes as an answer to the prophecy of the 70 years and as the ultimate solution. It is not just *a* messiah we are dealing with in this context, but *the* Messiah. Consulting the prophecy of the 70 years, Daniel expected one particular messiah, Cyrus. But the prophecy of the 70 weeks is the universal version of the prophecy of 70 years, as we see already implied in the language of the passage. The 70 years (7 x 10) lead to the messiah of the sabbatical year, whereas the 70 weeks, or "seventy sevens" (7 x 7 x 10), lead to a messiah of jubilee. Furthermore, words that in the context of Daniel's prayer expressed a particular and relative situation now appear in an indefinite and universal sense. For example, the word "transgression" *(ht')* in Daniel 9:24-27 has an indefinite sense (verse 24), whereas verses 1-23 employed the same word in a definite and particular sense: "We have sinned" (verses 5, 8, 11, 15), "our sins" (verse 16), "my sin" (verse 20), "the sin of my people" (verse 20). Likewise for the words "transgression," "justice," "vision," "prophecy," etc. It is thus not surprising, in this context, that the word "messiah" also has an indefinite, universal sense. And it is for the only time in the Hebrew Bible. The messiah in this passage is *the* Messiah, encompassing all other messiahs—the Messiah of messiahs, the universal Messiah.

The rest of the passage develops the mission of the Messiah as a universal one involving "many" (verse 27). In the biblical tradition the word *rabbim* (many) carries a strong universal connotation (see Ezra 3:12; Dan. 12:2). Prophets often use it to designate the peoples and the nations implicated in the universal adoration of God (Micah 4:2). The messiah in this passage is the Messiah of all peoples, the Messiah who will save the world.

And this is why this last Messiah leads to the jubilee, the Levitical festival symbolizing the re-creation of the world. It is a Sabbath of sabbaths, occurring every 7 x 7 years, a time of grace and liberty (Isa. 61:1, 2) when humanity and nature were born anew (Lev. 25:8-17).

But the prophecy of the 70 weeks is also related to the 2300 evenings and mornings. It was because Daniel felt troubled by the vision of 2300 evenings and mornings that was "beyond understanding" (Dan. 8:27) that he consulted the prophecy of 70 years to "understand" (Dan. 9:2), which later led to his vision of the 70 weeks to give him "insight and understanding" (verse 22). The key word "understand" is the golden thread woven through the passage. The prophecy of the 70 weeks provides the missing information necessary to understand the prophecy of the 2300 evenings and mornings. Moreover, the same angel, Gabriel, who had explained the prophecy of 2300 evenings and mornings, now reappears in chapter 9 to help Daniel "understand the vision" (verse 23). This same phrase with the same technical word "vision" *(mareh)* appears in the context of the prophecy of 2300 evenings and mornings (Dan. 8:16).

God sent the prophecy of the 70 weeks, proclaiming the coming of the Messiah, to help in "understanding" the prophecy of 2300 evenings and mornings. But the Messiah's coming is not mythical, something suspended above history. On the contrary, it is an event situated in time. A set of numbers given in the prophecy enable us to deduce a precise date. The numerical enigma of the prophecy is, we should warn our readers, especially challenging, and requires patience as well as effort.

We must clear up three things before we can chronologically decode the prophetic period: its beginning, duration, and conclusion. After that, we may discover the missing link between the prophecy of 2300 evenings and mornings and the prophecy of 70 weeks.

1. The Beginning

The appearance of the Messiah is the outcome of human words (*davar,* Dan. 9:25) announcing the restoration of Jerusalem that echo the divine words (*davar,* verse 23) answering Daniel's prayer. *Davar* (word) appears in both cases. In other words, the word from below that announces the reconstruction of Jerusalem is the answer to the word from above that inspires it. This word is the starting point of the prophetic 70-week period: "From the coming forth of a word to restore and reconstruct Jerusalem until the Messiah Prince, seven weeks and sixty-two weeks" (Dan. 9:25, literal translation).

The book of Ezra tells us that the city of Jerusalem would be rebuilt upon the proclamation of three successive decrees, one by Cyrus, a second by Darius, and the final one by Artaxerxes (Ezra 6:14). The first decree, issued in 538 by Cyrus, inaugurated the return of the first exiles. About 50,000 Jews returned to their land (Ezra 2:64). But the document essentially focused on the reconstruction of the Temple. It authorized the priests to bring back 5,400 cultic utensils that had formerly belonged to it (Ezra 1:11). The second decree, issued in 519 by Darius the First, Hystaspes (not Darius the Mede) only confirmed that of Cyrus (Ezra 6:3-12). Artaxerxes, otherwise known as Longimanus (long-armed, Ezra 7:13-26), promulgated the third royal decree. Several elements point to its being the "decree" mentioned by the prophecy:

1. It is the last decree, therefore the only effective one. In fact, Ezra uses the word "decree" in the singular to designate all three

decrees, as though to imply their common purpose.

2. This decree is the most thorough one, involving both the reconstruction of the Temple and the reestablishment of the political and administrative structures of Jerusalem (verse 25).

3. And finally, it is the only one to explicitly mention God's intervention: "Praise be to the Lord, the God of our fathers, who has put it into the king's heart to bring honor to the house of the Lord in Jerusalem in this way and who has extended his good favor to me. . . . Because the hand of the Lord my God was on me, I took courage and gathered leading men from Israel to go up with me" (verses 27, 28).

Significantly, this passage marks a transition from Aramaic, the language of exile, to Hebrew, the language of Israel. The decree of Artaxerxes introduces a linguistic shift, a sign both of a turning point in the history of Israel and the fact that the national restoration has indeed started. According to the book of Ezra, Artaxerxes would have issued his decree late in the seventh year of his reign (verse 8), that is, in early *fall* of 457 B.C.E.,[1] as Ezra left Babylon on the first day of the first month and arrived in Jerusalem on the first day of the fifth month (verses 8, 9). Therefore 457 is the point of departure of our prophecy.

2. The Duration

These weeks are prophetic. One day, therefore, corresponds to one year, which gives us week-years, rather than week-days.

1. Already the passage in Daniel confirms this. The period of the 70 years in Jeremiah in the introduction (verses 2, 3) echoes that of the 70 weeks in Daniel in the conclusion (verses 24-27). The two periods are related in a chiastic structure: the first phrase is "seventy years" (A B); the second phrase is formulated backwards, "weeks seventy" (B$_1$ A$_1$):

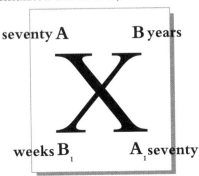

The chiasm already hints at the nature of those weeks by paralleling "seventy" with "seventy" and "years" with "weeks." Right from the start, the text of Daniel 9 should give us a directive as to what line of interpretation to follow: that we should read these weeks as weeks of years. Furthermore, immediately following chapter 9, the first words of chapter 10 directly confirm the interpretation given above. When it mentions three weeks of fasting, the text chooses to add the precise "three weeks of days" (verse 2, literal translation), the only occurrence in the whole Bible of such a careful distinction, as though to distinguish between two sorts of weeks: the week of years in Daniel 9 and the week of days in chapter 10.

2. The equation of "day-year" appears throughout the Bible. Narratives often employ the word "days" *(yamim)* in the sense of years to the point where most versions actually translate it by "years" (see Ex. 13:10; Judges 11:40; 1 Sam. 1:21; 2:19; 27:7; Num. 9:22; 1 Kings 11:42; Gen. 47:9, etc.). The poetic passages of the Bible contain many parallelisms between "days" and "years": "Are your days like those of a mortal or your years like those of a man?" (Job 10:5); "I thought about the former days, the years of long ago" (Ps. 77:5); "To proclaim the year of the Lord's favor and the day of vengeance of our God" (Isa. 61:2).

This principle also appears in Levitical texts. For six years the Israelite farmer was to work his land, but on the seventh year he had to let it be idle. Scripture calls the seventh year of rest a sabbath, like the seventh day of the week (Lev. 25:1-7), with the difference that it was a "Sabbath of years" and not a "Sabbath of days." The Bible uses the same language in regard to the jubilee: "Count off seven sabbaths of years—seven times seven years" (verse 8).

The principle also applied to prophecy. Hence, the 40 days during which the spies explored Canaan became 40 years of wandering in the desert. "For forty years—one year for each of the forty days you explored the land—you will suffer for your sins" (Num. 14:34). Likewise, God commanded the prophet Ezekiel to lie on his left side for so many days, each day symbolizing a year: "I have assigned you the same number of days as the years of their sin" (Eze. 4:5).

3. Both Jewish tradition and Christian tradition have understood

the weeks of Daniel as weeks of years. Among numerous works, we cite from the Hellenistic literature texts such as the Book of Jubilees (third/second century B.C.E.), the Testament of Levi (first century B.C.E.), 1 Enoch (second century B.C.E.); in the Qumran literature (second century B.C.E.) such texts as II Q Melchitsedeq, 4 Q 384–390 Pseudo-Ezekiel, the Damascus Document; in the rabbinical literature, texts such as the Seder Olam (second century C.E.), the Talmud, the Midrash Rabbah, and later the classical exegetes of the Middle Ages such as Saadia Gaon, Rashi, Ibn Ezra in the *Miqraoth Gdoloth*.[2] All testify since the most ancient times to the validity of our line of interpretation. The day-year principle of interpretation is probably the most ancient and the most solid principle in the exegesis of our passage.

Indivisible weeks. The vision's weeks of years are supposed to lead to the coming of the Messiah: "Until Messiah Prince seven weeks and sixty-two weeks . . . and after these sixty-two weeks shall be cut off the Messiah, and no one for him" (Dan. 9:25, 26; literal translation).

The coming of the Messiah is to occur after the 62 weeks that are added to the seven weeks. No break exists between the seven weeks and the 62 weeks, as some translations might imply. And yet the Masoretic text—that is, the text punctuated and vocalized by the Masoretes in the tenth century C.E. (our current Hebrew version)—indicates a disjunctive accent *(Athnakh)* that would indicate a break after "seven weeks." But several elements point to continuity.

1. The first reason is logical and contextual. Already the introduction sums up the weeks as 70: "Seventy 'sevens' are decreed for your people and your holy city" (verse 24). Furthermore, if we do not take the weeks in the sense of years, a rupture after seven weeks would be illogical, implying that the Messiah would come 49 years after 457 B.C.E. (seven times seven) instead of 483 years after that date (69 times seven).

2. The second reason is stylistic.[3] The biblical author has built the structure of the text upon the two entwined themes of the Messiah and Jerusalem, each with a distinctive key word. Each time the text refers to the Messiah (A_1, A_2, A_3), the word "weeks" *(shabuim)* appears, while each time the text speaks of Jerusalem (B_1,

B₂, B₃) the word "trench"/"decree" *(hrs)* appears. Notice the literary structure of Daniel 9:25-27 (literal translation):

    A₁   *Coming of the Messiah* (verse 25a)
        (since the going forth of the word to restore and build Jerusalem), to "the" Messiah Prince, 7 *weeks* and 62 *weeks*.

    B₁   *Construction of the city* (verse 25b)
        it will be restored and built with squares and *trenches* in a time of trouble.

    A₂   *Death of the Messiah* (verse 26a)
        after the 62 *weeks* he will be cut off without any help.

    B₂   *Destruction of the city* (verse 26b)
        and the people of the aggressive prince shall destroy the city and the sanctuary; its end shall be in a flood; until the end of the war *is decreed* desolations.

    A₃   *Covenant with the Messiah* (verse 27a)
        and he will strengthen a covenant with many for one *week;* and in the middle of the *week* he will cause sacrifice and offering to cease forever.

    B₃   *Destruction of the city* (verse 27b)
        and on the wing abominations, desolating until the end, and then what was *decreed* will be poured upon the desolating power.

Each time the same two key words appear in their respective contexts ("weeks" in the context of the Messiah, and "trench/decree" in the context of Jerusalem). Such a literary characteristic relates the seven and 62 weeks solely to the Messiah and not to Jerusalem (just as "trench/decree" is related to Jerusalem and not to the Messiah). Therefore, we infer from the structure that the break should come only after the 62 weeks (and not after the seven weeks), as is the case in the ancient translations such as the Septuagint Bible, the Syriac Bible, and even the Qumran version of the text.[4]

3. The third reason derives from the syntax and usage of the Masoretic disjunctive accent, the *athnach* attached to the word "seven." Indeed, the use of the *athnach* does not always mean separation. It is often used to mark an emphasis.[5] Thus in Genesis 1:1 the *athnach* is put under the verb *bara* (create) obviously not to mark a

separation between this verb and its complement object "heavens and earth" but rather to emphasize the divine operation of creation. Should the *athnach* be taken as a full disjunctive it would disturb the meaning of the sentence, making it read "In the beginning God created. The heaven and the earth." Another example appears in Genesis 22:10 in which the *athnach* is put on the word "knife," not to make a separation but to mark here also an emphasis, a pause expressing the idea that the knife is suspended. The effect of the *athnach* is not syntactical and should not be interpreted as marking a separation. It emphasizes the knife that threatens Isaac and thus suggests some kind of suspense. Likewise in Daniel 9:24 the *athnach* is put on the word "seven" to stress the importance of the number seven in the prophetic message. It is noteworthy, indeed, that the prophetic experience of Daniel starts (Dan. 9:2) with the vision of 70 years (7 x 10) and concludes with a vision of 7 weeks (7 x 7 x 10). Also symbolic is the way the 70 weeks are divided to again point out the number 7. It marks in Daniel 9:25 the beginning of the 70 weeks (7 weeks), and in verses 6-27, the end of the 70 weeks (1 week = 7 days). The reason for this emphasis on the number 7 is obviously to convey the ideas of completion and final salvation attached to the coming of the Messiah.

Therefore, the weeks of Daniel 9 constitute an indivisible sum. We should read the 62 weeks in conjunction with the 7 weeks. On the basis of the date of the beginning of the prophecy (457 B.C.E.) and its duration (70 weeks of years) it becomes possible to determine the end of the prophecy and to discover the event to which the prophecy leads.

3. The End of the Prophecy

His coming. The coming of the Messiah is then awaited for 69 weeks of years, that is, 483 years (69 x 7) from the point of departure, 457 B.C.E. The seventieth week would then be the year 27 of our era. The appearance of an individual called *"Christos"* (Greek rendition of the word Anointed/Messiah) would mark this year. It is precisely the year when Jesus was baptized and "anointed" by the Spirit (Luke 3:21, 22). Luke dates the event in the fifteenth year of the reign of Tiberius Caesar (verse 1).[6] Jesus inaugurated His ministry as Messiah by reading publicly from the text of Isaiah His own job description in terms of Jubilee: "The Spirit of the Lord is on me, because he has anointed me to preach good news to the poor. He has sent me to proclaim freedom for the prisoners and recovery of sight for the blind, to release the oppressed, to proclaim the year of the Lord's favor" (Luke 4:18, 19).

In mentioning the Jubilee, Jesus situates Himself directly in the perspective of the prophecy of the 70 weeks, which describes the same event also in terms of Jubilee (see above). Jesus thus defines Himself as the fulfillment of the prophecy: "And he began by saying to them, 'Today this scripture is fulfilled in your hearing'" (verse 21).

His death. The text of the prophecy goes as far as to predict the Messiah's death: "After the 62 weeks Messiah will be cut off. . . . In the middle of the week he shall make to cease sacrifice and offering" (Dan. 9:26, 27, literal translation).

The violence implied in the death of the Messiah the text renders by the verb "cut down" (*krt* in the *Niphal* form: passive). Interestingly, the verb in this form usually designates, in the legal parts of the Pentateuch, a person condemned to death. The verb is in a tense that implies a brutal and definitive action (Hebrew imperfect). But Scripture also describes the death of the Messiah in Levitical terms. The verb *krt* belongs to the context of the covenant made possible through the sacrifices. In Hebrew the verb *krt* always accompanies the word covenant (Gen. 15:18; Jer. 34:13), because in Hebrew, the covenant is cut *(krt)*. The word *krt* is rich in connotations of covenant and of the necessary sacrifice of the lamb (Gen. 15:10; Jer. 34:18).

In other words, Daniel announces the death of the Messiah in terms evocative of the covenant manifested by the death of the lamb in the Levitical system. The introduction of the prophecy of the 70 weeks already alludes to this by mentioning the atonement of sin (Dan. 9:24).

The prophecy thus identifies the Messiah with the sacrifice of the covenant. Like the lamb, His death made possible a covenant and assured divine forgiveness. All this was a language that the Israelites, living in a context where sacrifices were a part of daily life, could easily understand. The prophet Isaiah would use the same words in describing the suffering servant—representing neither Israel nor the prophet[7]—who must also die like a lamb in order to ensure forgiveness and salvation: "And the Lord has laid on him the iniquity of us all. He was oppressed and afflicted, yet he did not open his mouth; he was led like a lamb to the slaughter, and as a sheep before her shearers is silent, so he did not open his mouth" (Isa. 53:6, 7). It is thus not surprising that the Jews in the time of Jesus recognized the Messiah as "the Lamb of God, who takes away the sin of the world!" (John 1:29), and were able to discern in the daily sacrifices offered at the Temple a prefiguration of the Messiah-Saviour, "a shadow of the good things that are coming" (Heb. 10:1).

Consequently, His death should result in the annulling of the sacrifices: "And where these [sins] have been forgiven, there is no longer any sacrifice for sin" (verse 18), just as the prophet Daniel had predicted: "He will put an end to sacrifice and offering" (Dan. 9:27).

The death of the Messiah was then to occur in the *middle* of the seventieth week (verse 27). "Middle" is a better translation of the Hebrew term *hatsi* than "half," as some versions seem to infer. In certain contexts the word does mean "half," but in a situation involving a period of time it always means "middle," as is the case in our passage (see Ex. 12:29; Joshua 10:13; Judges 16:3; Ruth 3:8; Ps. 102:24). "In the middle of the week" signifies three years and a half after the year 27, that is the year 31, the year of the Crucifixion. The timing and the significance of the death of Jesus of Nazareth perfectly agree with the prophecy.

The fall of Jerusalem. Following the death of the Messiah, the prophet Daniel focuses on the destiny of Jerusalem and of the Temple: "And the people of the aggressive prince shall destroy the city and the sanctuary; its end shall be in a flood; until the end of the war is decreed, desolations . . . and on the wing abominations, desolating until the end, and then what was decreed will be poured upon the desolating power" (Dan. 9:26, 27, literal translation).

The prophecy is clear enough. It concerns the fall of Jerusalem and the destruction of the Temple but does not date the event. The 70-weeks prophecy restricts chronological data to the event of the

Messiah (see above). It only informs us that there will be "wars," "desolations," and "abominations," and that the tragedy will take place chronologically sometime after the Messiah's death.

A strong consensus in Jewish tradition recognizes that this prophecy refers to the Romans who "flooded" into the city and "devastated" the Temple, resulting in total "desolation." Flavius Josephus,[8] who apparently witnessed the event, the Talmud,[9] and the great medieval rabbis[10] Rashi, Ibn Ezra, etc., all agree that we should apply this prophetic vision to the siege of Jerusalem by the legions of Vespasian and finally by Titus in C.E. 70.

Note that the prophecy does not cite the event as God's punishment of His people. All the references to the history of Jerusalem (its reconstruction, as well as its destruction) serve as landmarks to situate the event of the Messiah. The Romans, however, it denounces as evil. The verb "destroy" (*yashhît* in Dan. 9:26) also appears in Daniel 8:24 with the evil power, the little horn, as its subject. Also the Romans are the direct object of the divine retribution that "will be poured upon them," language that implies God as the agent.

Now if the text implies a possible connection between the fall of Jerusalem and the sins of Israel, it never suggests the end of the Jewish people as it does for the Romans. It does mention the conclusion of the sacrificial system. And it does imply the termination of the Jewish theocracy, since the last Davidic king now sits on a heavenly throne. But the Jewish people survive and still keep worshiping and witnessing to the God of Abraham, Isaac, Jacob, and Daniel. Many among them recognized Jesus as their Messiah and thus brought the old testimony to distant parts of the world.

The covenant. It is noteworthy that the prophet Daniel does not describe the work of the Messiah as a "new covenant," but rather as a strengthening of the original covenant. The passage uses the word "confirm" (NIV) or "strengthen" (*higbir* from the root *gbr* denoting strength). The encounter with the Messiah was not designed to take the "new convert" outside of Israel, but on the contrary, it was supposed to strengthen his roots and his covenant with the God of Israel.

Moreover, this covenant concerns the *rabbim* ("many"), a technical term that connotes the idea of universiality.[11] The covenant is thus not only "strengthened" with "many" Jews, but is also extended to "many" nations. In contrast to the event of the fall of Jerusalem, this event is situated in time, for it concerns the Messiah: "He will strengthen covenant to many: one week"[12] (Dan. 9:27). The prophecy takes us then to that end of the last week of the 70 weeks (34 C.E.) It is noteworthy that the date marks an event that has had a considerable impact on civilization as well as being a key event for humanity's salvation. It was the year the message of the God of Israel explodes beyond the borders of Palestine and reaches the Gentiles, the "many" just mentioned (Acts 8). It is also the year of the conversion of Paul and of his commission from Christ (Acts 9). As well as the year God poured the Holy Spirit on Gentiles and Peter receives his strange vision urging him to preach to the Gentiles.

Yet many Christians, instead of paying attention to what the Messiah had done *on behalf* of the world, including and primarily the Jews (see Rom. 1:16), preferred to speculate and capitalize on what they thought He was doing *against* the Jews. Christians referred to the 70-weeks prophecy to justify the old visceral anti–Semitism. Ironically, the vision speaking of hope and love became the pretext for preaching about the "rejection of the Jews," "the divine curse on them," "God's ultimatum to Israel," etc., when nowhere does the text of the prophecy suggest such a concept. The New Testament does not support such a teaching. On the contrary, Paul asks, "Did God reject his people? By no means! I am an Israelite myself, a descendant of Abraham, from the tribe of Benjamin. God did not reject his people, whom he foreknew" (Rom. 11:1, 2). And a few verses further, the apostle refers to the rabbinic principle, *Akut Aboth* (the father's merits), to make the same point: "As far as election is concerned, they are loved on account of the patriarchs, for God's gifts and his call are irrevocable" (verses 28, 29). On the other hand, in the same chapter and speaking to those Christians who liked to boast and despised their Jewish roots, Paul warns: "Do not boast. . . . You do not support the root, but the root supports you" (verse 18). The apostle here discloses and denounces a driving force behind anti-Semitism: a spurning of Jewish roots. And because they themselves reject the Jews, such individuals involve God in their judgment and thus justify their theology by declaring that "God has rejected the Jews." By doing so, they identify themselves with God, a behavior that brings them close to the little horn of Daniel 7 and 8. In fact, by entertaining anti-Semitism, Christians, from whatever denomination, may be associating themselves with the oppressive little horn. In a sense, they become the little horn.

4. The Connection Between the Prophecies

God sent the 70-weeks prophecy not just to convince us about the historical event of the Messiah. For the prophet Daniel, we have seen, the vision of the 70 weeks serves the function of helping to better "understand" the vision of the 2300 evenings and mornings. Indeed, the two prophecies are situated in the same perspective and should be understood in relation to each other.

1. On the chronological level, the prophecy of the 70 weeks brings the missing link to the prophecy of the 2300 evenings and mornings: its starting point. The two prophecies commence with the same event, the decree of Artaxerxes in 457 B.C.E. However, the prophecy of the 70 weeks has its fulfillment sooner in the years 27, 31, and 34. That of the 2300 evenings and mornings covers a longer period. The technical expression "evening and morning," borrowed from the language of Creation, designates "a day." In our prophetic context one day means one year. Thus if we count 2300 years from 457 B.C.E., we reach the year 1844. But there is nothing more suspect and disturbing than a date, especially in religious matters. We feel more comfortable when religious truth remains within the limits of the spiritual domain. In Hebrew thinking, though, truth is not just a spiritual or a philosophical message designed only to nurture our souls and our minds. Instead, biblical truth is essentially historical. God speaks in history. And whatever explanation or whatever degree of emphasis we may want to give the date fulfilling this prophecy, we should not be surprised that biblical prophecy takes this risk of entering the flesh of history, even our modern history.

2. The two prophecies are related and complement each other in regard to their theological truth. Salvation takes two steps: first the

event of the cross, and second, the great cosmic atonement (2300 evenings and mornings), something already implied by Levitical ritual. The daily sacrifices were not enough. Kippur was also necessary to achieve complete salvation. The prophet Daniel already suggests such a necessity. All the key verbs of Daniel 8 and 9 are in the passive form *(Niphal)*, characteristic of Levitical language. Daniel 9 uses six verbs in the passive: "are decreed" (verse 24), "it will be rebuilt" (verse 25), "will be cut off" (verse 26), "have been decreed" (verse 26), "that is decreed" (verse 27), "is poured out" (verse 27). Daniel 8 employs only one verb in this form: "to consecrate" (verse 14). The verb in chapter 8 completes the other six in chapter 9, adding up to the sacred number of 7.

But Daniel 8 and 9 share yet another common element: the high priest. Daniel 9:24 and Exodus 29:36, 37 are the only two passages in the Bible with the three common themes of expiation, anointing, and the Holy of Holies. Without doubt Daniel had Exodus 29:42-44 in mind when transcribing his vision. The latter chapter describes the consecration of Aaron, the first high priest in Israel (verses 36, 37), and the institution of the daily sacrifice (verses 42-44). In this way, the prophecy of Daniel 9 links the atoning death of the Messiah to the consecration of the high priest and the daily sacrifice. Likewise, chapter 8 evokes the person of the high priest several times by the word "prince" (*sar,* technical term for the high priest of Israel; see 1 Chron. 15:22; Ezra 8:24; Dan. 10:5; and above).

However, the two prophecies are not situated in time in the same way. The second prophecy (Daniel 9) indicates the precise moment of the coming (anointing) of the Messiah. The first (Daniel 8) indicates the end of a period of time, given in answer to the question "How long?" (Dan. 8:13). The prophecy of the 70 weeks provides the precise date of an event while the prophecy of the 2300 evenings and mornings presents a duration after which there will be another event, that of the cleansing of the sanctuary (verse 14). The dating of the chapter 9 event is fixed, whereas the dating of the chapter 8 event remains open. The verbal forms expressing them render the difference between the two dates. A Hebrew imperfect (*yekaret:* "will be cut off," 9:26), which is a dynamic action, describes the death of the

Messiah. A Hebrew perfect (*nitsdaq:* "will be reconsecrated," 8:14) depicts the cleansing of the sanctuary. The death of the Messiah occurs in the year 31. It is a definite action, beginning and ending right there. The cleansing of the sanctuary, on the other hand, is an indefinite action extending beyond the year 1844 and which Daniel describes as "the time of the end" (see Dan. 8:17, 26).

This time of the end contains an event that we should furthermore understand in relation to the event occurring in the year 31. Many Christians have overlooked this aspect in their doctrine of salvation. The cross was enough, they declare. "All was accomplished." Christianity thus became a religion obsessed with the cross, a religion of the past and the present. It conceived of salvation as by works of holiness and of self-sacrifice patterned after the Great Example, or only a sentimental faith concerned with thinking and remembering the sacrifice of the Messiah. In any case, salvation *was*. The Christian religion had no need for the future, since the cross had already achieved salvation. Subjective experience came to replace the historical event. An existential religion prevailed over the biblical hope in the kingdom of God that promises that death and evil will then strike no more.

The cross without the kingdom makes no sense. Likewise, we need the event of the cross to survive the judgment. To save humanity, God had to descend into the wound of humanity, to die, and through His death, to save, to redeem us from our sin. Yet God does not merely want to show His love for us, as a hero would in a grandiose act of self-sacrifice, so that we may love and worship Him. Such a love would be quite self-centered. Because He truly loves, God wants to really save.

For death and evil to really cease, life must be overturned and all traces of sin wiped out. Salvation is more than an angelic act of grace—it is an act of violence against nature, against the elements. Such are the implications of judgment at the end of times.

3. Finally, on the existential level of the believer, faith in the redeeming sacrifice of the Messiah and hope in the kingdom of God depend on each other. The stronger the faith, the more intense the wait. Our existence is situated between the "now" and the "not

yet." In this state of tension life takes on new meaning. Hope in the future enriches the present. The good news of the gospel is that in spite of death and the sense we have of coming doom, we may still dream and expect something of the future.

Yet our wait for the new kingdom is not a passive one. Dynamic in nature, it stems from impatience, as was the case for Daniel. Ethical choice, the fight against injustice and suffering, all intensify during our wait. The future sheds light and perspective on the present. We see beyond immediate necessity and are no longer indifferent to the suffering of others. Because we think beyond our present condition, our decisions have a deeper foundation.

Despairing to ever understand, and worried by God's delay, Daniel falls to his knees in prayer. At the propitious moment of the evening offering, God's answer is a dying Messiah. In Daniel 7 the Messiah was the royal "son of man," who receives dominion over the world. Next in Daniel 8, the Messiah was the officiating high priest in Kippur attire. Finally, in Daniel 9 the Messiah is the atoning victim. The Hebrew mind plays the scenario backwards. For it is the death of the Messiah that serves as the basis for salvation (chapter 9). Then, brandishing the atoning power of this sacrifice, the Messiah pleads for us in the heavenly court and wins the trial (chapter 8). Finally, the kingdom is announced (chapter 7).

A song of death, the Requiem for the Messiah swells up in a crescendo of atonement and victory.

STRUCTURE OF DANIEL 9

I. **The Messiah of the seventy years (verses 1, 2)**
1. Year of the coming of Cyrus
2. Prophecy of Jeremiah

II. **Prayer (verses 3-19)**
  A Invocation of the Lord (verse 4)
    B We . . . (verses 5, 6)
      C Universal note (verses 7-9)
        a To you (verse 7)
          b To us (verse 7)
            c To all Israel (verse 7)

b_1 To us (verse 8)

a_1 To you (verse 9)

B$_1$ We . . . (verses 10-14)

A$_1$ Invocation of the Lord (verses 15-19)

III. The Messiah of the seventy weeks (verses 20-27)

70 weeks determined on the people and on Jerusalem (verse 24)

A$_1$ Coming of the Messiah: at the end of 7 and 62 weeks (verse 25a)

B$_1$ Construction of the city *(ḥrṣ)*

A$_2$ Death of the Messiah: after the 62 weeks (verse 26a)

B$_2$ Destruction of the city *(ḥrṣ)*

A$_3$ Covenant: middle of the week (verse 27a)

B$_3$ Destruction of destructor *(ḥrṣ)*

---

[1] History tells us that Artaxerxes began his reign in 465 B.C.E., the year of his ascending the throne (see "Artaxerxes," in *Universal Larousse*). According to the Bible, however, the first year of his reign would have begun at the beginning of the next year, in Tishri (see Jer. 25:1 and Dan. 1:1, 2; cf. 2 Kings 18:1, 9, 10; cf. Mishna *Rosh Hashanah* 1. 1). The seventh year of Artaxerxes would then extend from fall (Tishri) 458 to fall 457.

[2] See Jacques Doukhan, *Drinking at the Sources* (Mountain View, Calif.: Pacific Press, 1981), p. 67.

[3] See Jacques Doukhan, "The Seventy Weeks of Dan. 9: An Exegetical Study," 17, No. 1 (1979): 12-14.

[4] See Geza Vermes, *The Complete Dead Sea Scrolls in English* (New York: 1997), p. 127.

[5] See William Wickes, *Two Treatises on the Accentuation of the Old Testament* (New York: 1970), parts I:32-35; II:4.

[6] See Doukhan, *Drinking at the Sources,* pp. 135, 136, n. 186.

[7] For the distinction between the servant and Israel, see Isa. 49:5-7 and 53:4-6.

[8] Josephus, *Wars of the Jews,* 5. 6, 10.

[9] Babylonian Talmud *Gittin* 56a, 56b, 57b.

[10] *Miqraoth Gdoloth.*

[11] Doukhan, "The Seventy Weeks of Dan. 9," p. 21.

[12] Note that the word "for" generally used in our English translations does not appear in the Hebrew. In our literal translation from the Hebrew, the colon stands for the Masoretic disjunctive accent *tifha.*

CHAPTER 10

THE PRIEST
WITH EYES OF FIRE

Daniel 10:1 contains the book's last reference to Cyrus. It has already mentioned him twice: in the beginning (Dan. 1:21) and in the middle of the book (Dan. 6:28). The three last chapters "constitute a literary unit"[1] and occur in the same time span. We are in the third year of Cyrus (536/535), two years after chapter 9, which was dated in the first year of Darius, corresponding to the first year of Cyrus (see chapter 5).

The chapter begins on a stormy note. The first words proclaim a *tsava gadol,* a "great war" (verse 1). Daniel is still serving at the court of Babylon, and significantly, the book still calls him by his characteristic service name, Belteshazzar (verse 1). Just a year earlier he had witnessed the return of the exiles back to Jerusalem under the leadership of Sheshbazzar (Ezra 1:8). Daniel remained behind, however. It was too late for him. The weight of his 90 years kept him in the land of exile. The prophet of burning hope and ardent prayer was unable to participate in the fulfillment of his own prophecy (Dan. 9).

But his suffering involved more than mere nostalgia. In less than a year the deepest hopes of the prophet shattered. The vibrant chords of the song of Ezra have died out. Hostile silence greets the joyful cries of the returning exiles. Those left behind in the land hardly expected nor willed the return of the zealous refugees (Ezra 9:1, 2). Instead, they make every attempt to undermine the former exiles, employing discouragement, threats, accusatory letters to the

Persian authorities, and corrupting the officiating Temple priests (Ezra 4:4, 5). Their efforts jeopardized the rebuilding of the Temple. Hearts once ablaze with hope now bear the ashes of disillusionment. The news finally reached Daniel. Desperately he fell to his knees: "At that time I, Daniel, mourned for three weeks" (Dan. 10:2). That same anguish he had had two years before, when he had turned to the ancient prophecies of Jeremiah, gripped him again.

In fact, chapter 10 follows the same progression as chapter 9, a thematic correspondence brought out by the triadic structure of the two chapters. Both chapters begin with a despair that prophecy would not be fulfilled. In both Daniel acts out his grief in a gesture of contrition, and finally, in both cases, the angel Gabriel appears to explain.

I. Fasting on Passover

Daniel fasts for three weeks. Biblical tradition usually required only three days for the act of repentance (Ex. 19:10-15; Esther 4:16). Such is the intensity of his prayer that Daniel multiplies it by seven. Later Jewish tradition will retain the "three weeks" unit to commemorate the various tragedies that befell the Jewish people, especially the destruction of the Temple. This period of mourning, also called *beyn hametzarim* (literally "between the straits," meaning "in distress") takes place from the seventeenth of Tammuz to the ninth of Av (July-August).[2]

Daniel's prayer and fast takes place, however, in the first month of the year, Nisan, that is, precisely during the time of Passover and of the unleavened bread. He seems to allude to that fact as he feels the need to specify that "no meat or wine touched my lips" (Dan. 10:2), which would have been expected in the ritual meals of Passover. Jewish commentators have wondered about this irregularity that makes Daniel transgress the commandments of eating the lamb and the four cups of wine. They justify Daniel's decision, however, on the grounds that the interruption of the Temple's construction warranted such a response. We find a similar instance of a fast taking place on Passover in Esther 4:16.

A vision comes to Daniel on the twenty-fourth of Nisan, immediately after the week of Passover concludes (from the night of the fourteenth to the twenty-first). It is certainly not an accident that the vision occurs against the background of Passover, which celebrates the deliverance from Egypt and sets the mood for the Promised Land.

II. The Crushing Vision

And indeed the vision that catches Daniel reminds the reader of the one that surprised Joshua right after another Passover celebration (Joshua 5:10-12) as he prepared to enter Canaan. Both Joshua and Daniel introduce their visions with the exact same words: "I looked up and there before me was a man" (Dan. 10:5; cf. Joshua 5:13). The "man" of Joshua's vision identifies Himself as the "commander of the army," *sar hatsava* (Joshua 5:14, 15), an expression that appears only here and in Daniel 8:11, where the reference is to the heavenly High Priest in the context of the Day of Atonement. While the expression *sar hatsava* ("the commander of the army") does not occur as such in Daniel 10, yet both words recur separately in its context. The word *tsava* (army) crops up in the introduction of the chapter (Dan. 10:1) to provide the background and the perspective of the forthcoming revelation. And the word *sar* (prince) that designates the high priest in Daniel 8 here refers to Michael the fighting prince (Dan. 10:13, 21). Our text of Daniel 10 echoes then Daniel 8:11 and Joshua 5:14, 15. The "man" of Daniel's vision, the supernatural warrior of Joshua's vision, and the heavenly high priest of Daniel 8 are the same person. The vision confirms what the linguistic echoes suggest.

It is this High Priest that Daniel sees now in his magnificent apparel, complete with linen robe and gold belt (Dan. 10:5; cf. Lev. 16:4, 23; Ex. 28:4, 5, 8). This priest, however, looks different than any other priest. His whole being seems aflame. The passage compares His body to "chrysolite," *tarshish,* a precious stone coming from Tartessus, Spain, better known as topaz. The being's face shines like "lightning," and his arms and legs are "like the gleam of burnished bronze." The eyes flash like "flaming torches," and his voice projects "like the sound of a multitude."

Everything is in the superlative in an attempt to render the Priest's supernatural and extraordinary features. This kind of description appears elsewhere in Scripture. The book of Ezekiel mentions the same things: lightning (Eze. 1:14), chrysolite (verse 16), burnished bronze (verses 7, 27), fire (verses 13, 27), the voice like a multitude (verse 24). Ezekiel interprets it as "the appearance of the likeness of the glory of the Lord" (verse 28). This same being reappears in the book of Revelation, there also associated with the Passover feast[3] and also wearing the same priestly garment, the *poderes,*[4] with the golden sash (Rev. 1:13). There His eyes blaze like fire and His body resembles burnished bronze. Also His voice resounds like a multitude (verse 15). In that context, the being identifies Himself as divine: "I am the First and the Last. I am the Living One; I was dead, and behold I am alive for ever and ever! And I hold the keys of death and Hades" (verses 17, 18). The language used here clearly refers to Jesus Christ, described in the above verses as "firstborn from the dead" (verse 5), "the Alpha and the Omega" (verse 8). Moreover, Daniel's reaction, like that of Ezekiel and John, is one of terror (Dan. 10:9, 10; Eze. 1:28; Rev. 1:17). Such parallel imagery outside the book of Daniel indicates that he, like John and Ezekiel, sees a divine being and not just an angel. Even Gabriel does not inflict such terror (Dan. 9:21).

The book of Daniel itself identifies the being as the "son of man" of Daniel 7:13. Daniel 10:4 uses the ambiguous term "man" to describe Him, a fact further confirmed by the book of Revelation, which explicitly identifies the being depicted in Daniel 10 as the "son of man" of Daniel 7 (Rev. 1:13). Thus the son of man of chapter 7, the Prince "High Priest" in chapter 8, and our fiery being in chapter 10 all represent the same God-man person who had so terrified Daniel, Ezekiel, and John.

Overwhelmed by his extraordinary vision, the prophet is too disturbed to even try to understand. Now the familiar angel Gabriel intervenes to strengthen and comfort Daniel, and to help him understand.

III. The Comforting Vision

In verse 9 the vision switches from sight to sound as Gabriel gives Daniel "insight and understanding" (cf. Dan. 8:17-19; 9:21-23). The messenger from above presents himself in the same terms as those used in chapter 9. "Since the first day that you set your mind to gain understanding and to humble yourself before your God, your words were heard, and I have come in response to them" (Dan. 10:12).

Daniel had barely begun his prayer when already his words were heard. His three weeks of praying and fasting were not even necessary. From the first day God had heard his prayer. Scripture does not record the words of such a lengthy prayer, as though to remind the reader of the little value words have before God. The Lord hears the prayer before it is even formulated, let alone embellished by words. The content of prayer is more important than the form it takes. The words have no power per se. It reminds us of the story of a very pious man who, upon forgetting all his prayers, rushes to the rabbi and cries: "I have forgotten how to pray! What am I to do?" To which the rabbi answers: "Don't worry, just recite the alphabet and the angels will compose for you the most beautiful of prayers." A child's stuttering sometimes speaks louder than the elaborate and eloquent invocations of the great professionals of prayer. God's answer depends on neither the quantity nor the quality of words.

But yet another lesson lies hidden behind the angel's words. During the 21 days that Daniel spent praying, Gabriel had been engaged in a struggle with "the prince of the Persian kingdom" (verse 13)—as though the spiritual struggle experienced by Daniel was somehow related to the conflict between the earthly kingdoms. Daniel's prayer, which seemed to us so small and futile, had in fact cosmic repercussions. In a way Gabriel seems to contradict himself. On the one hand, he implies that Daniel's prayer was wasted, while on the other he admits that it supported him for 21 days in his struggle with the prince of Persia.

The relation between these two truths seems contradictory and mysterious. The pious works of humanity are worth nothing in and of themselves, but God wills them to affect the course of history. God has chosen to need humans. Only such downward movement of God, binding heaven to earth, allows hope and faith to subsist. Life takes on meaning in spite of its absurdities and accidents. In spite of its contingency, existence remains in the divine hands. He will always have the last word.

Gabriel's revelation developed in two successive stages, each one parallel to the other, and ending on the same evocation of Michael, the allied angel from above.

A (verse 9)	A_1 (verse 15)
Daniel hears the words; falls to the ground.	Daniel hears the words; falls to the ground.
B (verses 10, 11)	B_1 (verses 16, 17)
The angel touches the hands and knees of Daniel, who stands up trembling.	The angel touches the lips of Daniel, who opens his mouth to speak with difficulty.
C (verse 12)	C_1 (verses 18, 19)
The angel comforts him: "Do not be afraid."	The angel comforts him: "Do not be afraid."
D (verse 13)	D_1 (verses 20, 21)
Battle with the prince of Persia, with Michael as an ally.	Battle with the prince of Persia, with Michael as an ally.

Twice Daniel senses in his body the transition from life to death (A B // A_1 B_1). And twice he receives comfort. The battle against Persia follows its course in history according to the prophecy (verse 20), since Greece (Javan) is soon to make its entry on the historical scene (verse 20).

Gabriel's message is one of victory. Already the angel's name itself hints at this. "Gabriel" derives from the verb *gbr* (to be strong) and belongs to the vocabulary of warfare,[5] providing the origin for the word *gibbor*, the war hero.[6]

And indeed, at the climax of his discourse (D // D_1), Gabriel emits the battle cry: "Michael!"—Who is like God? (Mi-ka-el). Biblical tradition presents it as the battle cry of a people in awe at the victorious intervention of their God in battle: "The enemy boasted, 'I will pursue, I will overtake them. . . . I will draw my sword and my hand will destroy them.' But you blew with your breath, and the sea covered them. . . . *'Who* among the gods *is like you,* O Lord? *Who is like you*—majestic in holiness?'" (Ex. 15:9-11).

The same cry of victory permeates the Psalms: "My whole being will exclaim, *'Who is like you,* O Lord? You rescue the poor from those too strong for them'" (Ps. 35:10). And the prophets: "This is what the Lord says—Israel's King and Redeemer, . . . *Who then is like me?* . . . Let him foretell what will come" (Isa. 44:6, 7).

Gabriel mentions Mi-ka-el as one fighting on his side (Dan. 10:13, 21) and as the prince of Daniel and his people (verse 21). Verse 13 hints at a superlative: *"The* chief prince" (literal translation) and not "one of the chief princes" (NIV). The word *ahad,* usually translated as the number "one," also means "first."[7] The latter meaning fits the phrase and the book of Daniel better.

The author uses the word *ahad* ("one" or "first") instead of the word *rishon* ("first") to avoid the otherwise redundant *rishon ha rishonim,* "first of firsts." In general, the book of Daniel employs *ahad* rather than *rishon* to render "first."[8] The superlative "first of the first princes" designating Michael is the equivalent of the expression "Prince of princes" of Daniel 8:25 and refers, therefore, to the same supernatural figure.

The priest with eyes of fire who had terrorized Daniel is in fact Michael—the son of man of chapter 7 and the Prince of princes of chapter 8. In chapters 7 and 8 the being had appeared only after the long and tumultuous history of the kingdoms born of the waters, symbol of nothingness and darkness. But in chapter 10 the revelation takes an abrupt shortcut. Bypassing the kingdoms, the being appears immediately upon the waters.

It is as if we had already reached the last stage of the coming of the "Son of man." Standing on the water, Michael looks, indeed, familiar. He is the one who concludes the line of the beasts in chapter 7 and in chapter 8. But he is also the one who stood before Joshua on the plain of Jericho, carried Israel across the Jordan River, fought for them, and led them finally into the Promised Land.

As the angel informs Daniel of the impending "great political war between kingdoms" (see Dan. 10:1, 20) and the more serious spiritual and cosmic war between good and evil, the vision brings hope of victory.

The authors of the New Testament have identified this being—the priest with flaming eyes, the Son of man—as Jesus Christ, the glorious judge who arrives seated upon the clouds (Rev. 1:13-18) and high priest officiating in the heavenly temple (Heb. 7:5-10 and 9:11-15). The ancient rabbis followed a similar line of thought and saw Michael as the awaited *Mashiach* and the high priest officiating in the heavenly Zion.[9]

STRUCTURE OF CHAPTER 10

Introduction (verse 1)

    1. Last mention of Cyrus

    2. Construction of temple compromised

I. Tishri on the Tiger (verses 2, 3)

Three weeks of fasting and praying

II. The overwhelming vision (Michael) (verses 4-8)

    1. The great priest (cf. Eze. 1; Rev. 1)

    2. Daniel in deep sleep

III. The enlightening vision (Gabriel) (verses 9-21)

    A   Words heard, prostration (verse 9)

        B   Strengthened by the angel (verses 10, 11)

            C   Encouraged by the angel (verse 12)

                D   Battle against Persia with Michael (verses 13, 14)

    A_1 Words heard, prostration (verse 15)

        B_1 Strengthened by the angel (verses 16, 17)

            C_1 Encouraged by the angel (verses 18, 19)

                D_1 Battle against Persia with Michael (verses 20, 21)

---

[1] Lacocque, *The Book of Daniel,* p. 200.

[2] Counting from the first month, Nisan, Zechariah 8:19 refers to these fasts respectively as Tammuz (fourth month) and Av (fifth month).

[3] See Doukhan, *Le cri du ciel,* pp. 40-42.

[4] It is the only occurrence of this Greek word in the New Testament. The Septuagint Bible, however, uses it to refer to the specific dress of the high priest (in the Septuagint Bible, see Ex. 25:6, 7; 28:4; Eze. 9:2, 3, 11, etc.; cf. also *Antiquities,* 3. 153ff; cf. Irenaeus *Adv Haer* 4, 20).

[5] Ex. 17:11; 1 Sam. 2:9; 2 Sam. 1:23; Job 21:7; Isa. 42:13, etc.

[6] 1 Sam. 14:52; Isa. 3:2; Jer. 46:12; Eze. 39:20; Zech. 9:13; Ps. 33:16, etc.

[7] Gen. 1:5; Ex. 40:2; Lev. 23:24; Deut. 1:3; 1 Kings 16:23; 2 Chron. 29:17; Ezra 1:1; 3:6; 7:9; 10:16, 17; Eze. 26:1; 29:17; 31:1, etc.

[8] The book of Daniel has six uses of the word *ahad* meaning "first" (Dan. 1:21; 9:1, 2; 11:1; 6:2; 7:1) versus four uses of the word *rishon* (Dan. 8:21; 10:4, 12, 13). This tendency appears in most postexilic literature because of the influence of Aramaic.

[9] See Babylonian Talmud *Zebahim,* 62a; Babylonian Talmud *Menahoth* 110a; *Midrash Rabbah* of Exodus 18:5; *Midrash on the Psalms,* Psalm 134, section 1; *Pesikta Rabbati,* Piska 44, section 10; etc.

CHAPTER 11

WORLD WARS

T he vision of Michael reassured Daniel. A thunderous moment of truth revealed the victorious outcome of the cosmic war. Presently, the angel Gabriel elaborates on the
conflict itself. We enter the chapter of warfare. Conflict
appears like a leitmotiv in the book of Daniel, rumbling in the
background to finally explode in our present chapter. Up to now
we had heard it only in a somewhat muted form ranging from the
Babylonian victory over Jerusalem in chapter 1 (Dan. 1:2) to the
conflict between the ruler of Babylon and the Hebrews, servants of
God (chapters 3 and 6). Later, we find it in the opposition between
the human and the beastly (Dan. 2:34, 44; 4:15, 23, 32, 33; 7:13,
14; 8:11, 25). In chapter 9 the conflict took on a universal note
with the evocation of the Messiah of messiahs, whose violent death
the vision announces. Finally, in chapter 10, the conflict openly
breaks out as a "great war" (*tsava gadol* [verse 1]). Daniel's personal
struggle and fast have their parallel in a battle involving supernatural powers, suggesting the cosmic and spiritual nature of the upcoming conflict. Now in chapter 11 we penetrate the essence of
this warfare.

The first words, immediately following those of chapter 10, send
us back to the era of Darius the Mede when Daniel had received his
vision of the 70 weeks (Dan. 9:1). It is in the perspective of Messianic
hope that we may now tackle the stormy events of chapter 11.

I. The Persian Wars

The angel Gabriel retells the story from the start. He goes back to the time of the "first year of Darius" (Dan. 11:1). Significantly, the prophecy zooms in on none other than Artaxerxes the Persian, identified in our commentary (see above) as the starting point of the prophecy of 70 years and of the 2300 evenings and mornings. "Three more kings will appear in Persia, and then a fourth, who will be far richer than all the others. When he has gained power by his wealth, he will stir up everyone against the kingdom of Greece" (verse 2).

The three kings are of Persian origin. We are in the reign of Cyrus (with coregent Darius). Thus the three kings would be Cambyses (530-522), Darius (522-486),[1] Xerxes, the Ahasuerus of Esther (486-465), with the fourth being Artaxerxes (465-423). Not only did Jewish tradition adopt the interpretation,[2] history also confirms it. Artaxerxes was, as depicted in the prophecy, extremely rich. A history text describes him as the king who "was shrewdest (of all his predecessors) and bought off his allies (from the conquered Greek cities), weakening them by creating dissension among them."[3]

The mention of Artaxerxes at the dawn of the great conflict is particularly significant. It is he who marked the starting point of the 70-weeks and the 2300-evenings-and-mornings prophecies. Just as God led history until the coming of the Messiah in chapter 9, and until the time of the end in chapter 8, likewise He will do so for the great forthcoming conflict.

The king mentioned after Artaxerxes is easy to recognize. The language of the angel in verses 3 and 4 is the same as in Daniel 8:8: "The goat became very great, but at the height of his power his large horn was broken off, and in its place four prominent horns grew up toward the four winds of heaven."

"Then a mighty king will appear, who will rule with great power and do as he pleases. After he has appeared, his empire will be broken up and parceled out toward the four winds of heaven" (Dan. 11:3, 4).

We are thus dealing with Alexander the Great, whose empire his four generals subsequently divided "to the four winds of heaven" upon his death. The totality of the Greek kingdom, including its colonies, is included in the word "empire" (*malkuth* [verses 2, 4]) as was also the case with the Persian kingdom (Dan. 10:13). The next phrase is more difficult to understand. It literally reads: "And not in its hereafter, and not according to the domination which ruled it, for its kingdom shall be torn and (handed over) to others than these" (Dan. 11:4).

In other words, we are witnessing here a transition of power as the "kingdom" *(malkuth)* passes over to "others than these." The plural form of "these" *(elleh)* relates it to the four winds of heaven, also in the plural form.[4] The kingdom then comes under the control of a power that arises after the division of the Hellenistic empire. This new power, as we have seen in the earlier prophecies, is Rome.

Certain commentators interpret the expression "these" as referring to generals other than the four mentioned above. They think then of the dynasties of Armenia and Cappadocia that regained their independence 150 years after the death of Alexander.[5] Such an interpretation does not fit the biblical text. As far as Armenia and Cappadocia were concerned, they involved only part of the empire, yet the biblical narration clearly mentions the "four winds of heaven," implying hereby the totality of the empire. Clearly, the prophecy has the kingdom of Rome itself in mind.

As in chapter 8, Daniel 11 barely alludes to the kingdom of Rome and focuses on the next stage that will last until "the time of the end" (verse 40).

II. North Versus South

The events introduced in verse 5 come chronologically after Rome and do not apply to the Hellenistic kingdoms of the Ptolemies and the Seleucids, as the traditional line of interpretation infers.[6] The period covered by the conflict narrated in Daniel 11:5–45 is therefore the same as that covered by the little horn in Daniel 7 and 8, and by the toes in Daniel 2. This is already implied by the structural parallelism between chapters 8 and 11. The section concerning the little horn in chapter 8 matches the section concerning the north-south conflict in chapter 11.

Chapter 8	Chapter 11
Persia (verses 3, 4)	Persia (verse 2)
Greece (verses 5-8)	Greece (verses 3, 4)
Rome (verses 8, 9)	Rome (verse 4)
Little horn (verses 9-12)	North-south conflict (verses 5-39)
Time of the end (verses 13, 14, 17, 25)	Time of the end (verses 40-45)

It must be added that the northern power as described in chapter 11 has much in common with the little horn, even down to linguistic similarities:

1. The king of the north challenges God and seeks to usurp Him (Dan. 11:36, 37). In chapter 8 the little horn rises to the heavenly hosts (verses 10, 11) against the "Prince of princes" (verse 25).

2. The king of the north desecrates the sanctuary and abolishes the daily sacrifice (Dan. 11:31), while in Daniel 8 the little horn desecrates the sanctuary (verse 11) and takes away the daily sacrifices (verse 12).

3. The king of the north establishes himself in the "Beautiful Land"[7] *(tsevi),* an expression symbolizing Palestine (Dan. 11:16, 41, 45), and attacks the holy covenant (verses 28, 30). The little horn grows toward the "Beautiful Land" (Dan. 8:9) and destroys the "holy people" (verse 24).

4. Like the king of the north, the little horn of chapter 8 originates from the north (verse 9).

5. The king of the north and the little horn die the same death. The king of the north comes to his end without the help of anyone (Dan. 11:45), while the little horn "will be destroyed, but not by human power" (Dan. 8:25; cf. 2:45).

The power of the north and the little horn therefore present the same characteristic features, the same behavior, come from the same direction, and share the same tragic death. Finally, they cover the same time span, extending from the fall of the Roman Empire to the time of the end. We then conclude that the king of the north and the little horn represent the same power, one enjoying political recognition and exercising divine prerogatives. The story of the north-south conflict in Daniel 11:5-45 is the same as that of the little horn in chapter 8. We now must discover the meaning of this conflict and its historical implications.

1. A Spiritual Meaning

Both the literary structure of the text and the symbolism of the north-south reference imply the conflict's spiritual nature.

The literary structure. From verse 5 the narration develops in six sections. The first three (verses 5-12: A, B, C) are symmetrical to the last three (verses 13-39: A_1, B_1, C_1). The two parts ABC and A_1 B_1 C_1 reflect each other thematically (same themes) and linguistically (same words and expressions). Moreover, the attacks of the two powers alternate (A south; B north; C south; A_1 north; B_1 south; C_1 north). When A refers to the south, A_1 refers to the north and so forth.

A south (verses 5-8)	A_1 north (verses 13-25a)
With great *(rab)* power (verse 5)	With a huge *(gadol)* army and much *(rab)* equipment (verse 13)
Alliances *(yesharim)* between the south and the north (initiated by the south) (verse 6)	Alliances *(yesharim)* between the north and the south (initiated by the north) (verse 17; cf. 22, 23)
Alliance fails *(lo yaamod)* (verse 6)	Alliance fails *(lo taamod)* (verse 17)
A daughter *(bat)* is given (verse 6)	A daughter *(bat)* is given (verse 17)
Standing at his place *(we amad . . . kanno)* and will enter his fortress *(maoz)* (verse 7)	Standing at his place *(we amad al kanno)* will turn back toward the fortresses *(maoz)* (verses 18-25a)

B north (verses 9, 10)	B₁ south (verses 25b-27)
A great army *(hayil)* (verse 9)	A large army *(hayil)* (verse 25)
The sons of the king of the north will prepare for war *(yitgare)* against the realm of the king of the south (verse 10)	He will stir up his strength *(yitgare)* against the king of the north (verse 25)
Sweep on like a flood *(shtf)* (verse 10)	Army swept away like a flood *(shtf)* (verse 26)
C south (verses 11, 12)	**C₁ north (verses 28-39)**[8]
The king['s heart] *(leb)* will be filled with pride (verse 12)	But his heart *(leb)* will be set up (verse 28)
Will slaughter many thousands *(ribboth)* (verse 12)	And many *(rabbim)* will join them (verse 34)

The rest of chapter 11 concerns the "time of the end." Verses 40-45 are set apart from the rest of the chapter as the concluding statement. There also, the conflict follows a given structure:

1. The south attacks the north (verse 40a)
2. The north attacks the south (verse 40b)

→ partial victory against the "Beautiful Land" (verse 41)

3. The north attacks the south (verses 42, 43a)
4. The south allies with the north (verse 43b)

→ attack against the "holy mountain" from above: supernatural end of the king of the north, "no one will help him" (verses 44, 45); victory.

The symmetry and structure of these passages warn against a strictly literal and historical interpretation. We are dealing with a stylistic technique suggesting more than the event per se, but rather what it intends to symbolize.

The north-south symbolism. Significantly, starting with

verse 5, the two kingdoms are no longer explicated, as had been the case up to now (Persia, Greece). The allusions to the north and south become abstract and metaphorical.

Elsewhere the Bible uses the unit "north-south" to express the idea of totality and earthly space.[9]

"The heavens are yours, and yours also the earth; you founded the world and all that is in it. You created the north and the south" (Ps. 89:11, 12).

"This is what the Lord says: I am against you. I will draw my sword from its scabbard and cut off from you both the righteous and the wicked. . . . My sword will be unsheathed against everyone from south to north" (Eze. 21:3, 4).[10]

Taken separately, the references to the north, as to the south, have their own meanings. The north is the biblical representative of evil, which usurps God. The little horn comes from the north. Likewise, the prophets identified evil and tragedy as coming from the north:

"Melt away, all you Philistines! A cloud of smoke comes from the north, and there is not a straggler in its ranks" (Isa. 14:31).

"From the north disaster will be poured out on all who live in the land" (Jer. 1:14).

The language has its origin in the threat posed by the Babylonian armies that came up over the "Fertile Crescent" and down from the north. Babylon, the great usurper, quickly assimilated into the imagery of the north.

"The Lord Almighty, the God of Israel, says: 'I am about to bring punishment on Amon god of Thebes, on Pharaoh, on Egypt and her gods and her kings, and on those who rely on Pharaoh. I will hand them over to those who seek their lives, to Nebuchadnezzar king of Babylon and his officers'" (Jer. 46:25, 26).

The link between Babylon and the north finds further confirmation in ancient Middle Eastern literature. In Canaanite mythology the god of Baal dwelled in the north. The reference to the north, be it through Baal or Babylon, carries religious implications and allusions to the usurpation of God. Isaiah composed his epic on the king of Babylon with these ideas in mind:

"You said in your heart, 'I will ascend to heaven; I will raise my throne above the stars of God; I will sit enthroned on the mount of assembly, on the utmost heights of the sacred mountain [or *the north;* Hebrew *Zaphon*]. I will ascend above the tops of the clouds; I will make myself like the Most High'" (Isa. 14:13, 14).

A similar allusion to Babylon appears in the book of Revelation calling the little horn, usurper of God, "Babylon" (Rev. 14:8; 16:19; 17:5; 18:2, 10, 21).

On the other hand, the south symbolizes, in the biblical tradition, human power without God. The south symbolizes Egypt (Dan. 11:43), especially Pharaoh in his proud rejection of God: "Who is the Lord, that I should obey him. . . . I do not know the Lord" (Ex. 5:2).

The prophets considered an alliance with Egypt as a displacement of faith from God to humanity—faith in humanity replacing faith in God. "Woe to those who go down to Egypt for help, who rely on horses, who trust in the multitude of their chariots and in the great strength of their horsemen, but do not look to the Holy One of Israel, or seek help from the Lord. . . . But the Egyptians are men and not God; their horses are flesh and not spirit" (Isa. 31:1-3).[11]

On the one hand, we have the north representing religious power striving to usurp God, while on the other, we have the south standing for human endeavors that reject God and have faith in humanity alone.

Such references to the north and to the south were well known to the average Israelite and were an integral part of the nation's history. Sandwiched between Egypt and Babylon, Israel came to understand and imagine its destiny strictly in relation to these two dominant forces. Thus it is not surprising that Daniel should use the traditional references to the north and to the south in describing the destiny of God's people. Already the allusion to the little horn testifies to the spiritual character of the conflict. The book of Daniel always depicts this power in symbolic language. In Daniel 2 clay, symbol of the human, represents it. Daniel 7 and 8 have a little horn with human features. We have already seen how human characteristics render the spiritual in the book of Daniel.

We should understand both the conclusion of the chapter (verses 40-45) and the preceding development (verses 5-40) in a symbolic sense. They have the same poetic language of regularity and of symmetry in speaking of the northern and southern powers, both of which are involved in the conclusion as well as in the development. We are dealing with the same king of the north: "The king of the South will engage him in battle" (verse 40). The "him" is the king of the north, mentioned in the preceding verses. We should therefore understand the north-south reference in a symbolic sense all the way through, not only from verse 40 to the end, but also before verse 40, that is, from verse 5 on.

Its development in seven stages (the seventh stage being the time of the end) further supports the allegorical or symbolic aspect of the narration. From A_1 on, however, the north-south antagonism couples itself with the parallel conflict between the north and the people of God.

In A_1 verses 16 and 20 described the conflict as a battle led by the north against the "Beautiful Land," an idiomatic expression designating Palestine, location of the Temple (Zech. 7:14; Eze. 20:6, 15),[12] thus understood in a religious sense, and not simply in a geographical sense.

In C_1 the conflict breaks out again in verses 30-32 through the aggression of the north against the holy covenant, the sanctuary, and God's people. Underneath the parallelism and the symbols, the text hints at a chronological progression and a somewhat obscure historical development.

2. A Historical Meaning

It is not easy to find the historical counterpart to our passage. At this stage of our research, it is, however, still possible to outline three main themes in verses 5 to 39.

The theme of conflict between the north and the south. This may refer to the conflict that traditionally opposed two inexorable enemies: On one hand, the religious ecclesiastical power (the north) plays the role of God on earth, acting as sole intercessor between wretched humanity and God. On the other hand, the philosophical and political movements (the south) fight against obscurantism and fanaticism with the weapon of reason. Both movements constantly wage war with each other. We see this unending struggle displayed in the attacks of the Neoplatonists, the persecutions of the pagan emperors (Nero, Diocletian, Julian, etc.), the humanistic currents born of the Renaissance, the French Revolution, and finally in our present ideologies and secular and materialistic forms of government.

The theme of alliance between the north and the south in verses 6, 17, 22, 23. We think of the attempts of compromise between the church and the state of Constantine, the medieval alliances on questions of law, territorial control, power, and philosophy, and the many religio-political forces at work in the present.

The theme of conflict between the north and the people of God in verses 16, 28, 30, 31, 35. Persecution and intolerance has marked the history of the church from the fourth century to the French revolution,

The literary form of our text, particularly its symmetry, warns us against a literalistic interpretation of the details. These three themes pave the way for the events at the end of time. For now, the north-south conflicts, their alliances, and the attacks of the north against God's people have been mere preliminaries. We must wait for the last phase, concerning the time of the end (verses 40-45), to really grasp the full significance behind these conflicts and alliances. The passage speaks from the perspective of the end, outlining in the development (verses 5-40) only those themes relevant to the time of the end. Only at the conclusion of the narration will we be somewhat able to grasp the significance of the three themes outlined in the development.

This last battle occurs in two offensives, each one involving some sort of attack against God's people.

1. We witness first an attack of the south against the north. The battle is short but intense with the south being crushed by the north: "storm[ing] out against him with chariots and cavalry and a great fleet of ships" (verse 40). This first massive victory precedes the final victory of the north. He attains at last the "Beautiful Land," but victory is not yet total: "Many countries will fall, but Edom, Moab and

the leaders of Ammon will be delivered from his hand" (verse 41).

Historically, it means that the politico-religious power will triumph over the atheistic and political movements. During the heat of the action, attempts will be made against the people of God. Yet, if we believe Daniel, the north's victory is neither total nor definitive. In its symbolic language, the prophecy suggests a southern resistance pushing from Edom, Moab, and Ammon.[13] This means that the various atheistic and humanistic movements will resist and for a moment prevail over religious forces.

2. But the prophecy of Daniel looks yet further. A second offensive takes place. The king of the north penetrates into the most southern regions of the south: Egypt, Libya, and Ethiopia. But rumors from the northeast, that is, from Palestine (if we consider him to be in Ethiopia at that time) force him to return in that direction. He sets out in a "great rage" (verse 44). His intentions are clear: to "destroy and annihilate." Occupied with southern conquests, he had up to now neglected such marginal disturbances. Now nothing holds him back anymore. No longer alone, his enemies now march at his side (verse 43). For the first time, the north and the south are allied. The peoples of the south (Libyans, Ethiopians, and Egyptians) recognize the north as their leader and follow him into the last battle, against the "beautiful holy mountain." They erect their camp "between the seas" (verse 45), that is between the Mediterranean Sea and the Dead Sea, which frame the land of Israel.[14] Their appearance threatens the Temple of God. In biblical language, the "beautiful holy mountain" designates the location of the Temple, and by extension, the Temple itself.[15]

It is the Temple that makes the land sacred and beautiful *(tsevi)*. Such a land can be described only in poetic terms, for beyond its landscape the poet of Israel senses the holy dimensions of God's dwelling place. The psalmist (Ps. 48:1, 2) assimilates the "holy mountain" to the "utmost heights of Zaphon" (the extreme north), an idiomatic expression designating the heavenly heights of God's dwelling place (see Isa. 14:13). We find a similar usage in Solomon's dedication of the Temple: "May your eyes be open toward this temple night and day, this place of which you said, 'My Name shall be there,' so that you will hear the prayer your servant prays toward this place. Hear the supplication of your servant and of your people Israel when they pray toward this place. Hear from heaven, your dwelling place" (1 Kings 8:29, 30). The Israelite would then address his prayers toward the Temple, residence of God's name, and from heaven, God's dwelling place, would come the answer.

The expression "beautiful holy mountain" of Daniel 11:45 is then the heavenly location of God's dwelling. Already Daniel 2 mentioned such a mountain and in the context of the end, specifically during the earthly kingdoms' last attempts to unite (Dan. 2:35, 44, 45). We find the same elements in Revelation 16's famous prophecy of Armageddon. It also characterizes the time of the end by the union of the "kings of the whole world" (verse 14).

The Armageddon of the book of Revelation, as well as the mountain in the book of Daniel, should not be understood as a geographical location, but as an allusion to a spiritual battle of cosmic dimensions. We must especially keep this in mind as we consider the mountain's historical implications. According to Daniel 2 and Revelation 16, "all the kings of the earth," that is, both the north and the south (Daniel 11), unite for the first time in a battle of spiritual implications. Their mutual target is the throne of God, the kingdom of God. While this may seem a little far-fetched to some, a look at what is happening in the world these days should convince us of the prophetic truth.

No one believes in the kingdom of God anymore. Many treat with condescension this hope of the early Christians, the very essence of Christianity.[16] Too many Christians have today integrated into their beliefs humanistic and materialistic ideologies. Instead of looking toward the soon-to-come City of God, they work at building it here and now. The focus has shifted to human enterprise. Today religion follows the footsteps of socialist and existentialist trends of justice, love, and happiness and leaves God out. We find it in the liberation theology of the underdeveloped countries of the world and the dream of Teilhard of Chardin, who promises "singing tomorrows." It is also the dialectic of Bultmann, who limits the wait for the kingdom of God to individual existential experience, thus eliminating God from the historical arena. Such theologians no longer define the kingdom of God in terms of historical reality. We prefer the more elegant terms of evolution, progress, and enlightenment. Faith becomes more realistic. The church has never been so politically involved as today. Since the fall of Communism, the voice of the church has again become audible in the countries of eastern Europe. Likewise, right-wing extremism in the capitalist West attempts to combine religion and politics.

Traces of the same mentality appear in the Islamic world. Extremist movements proliferate everywhere, including Morocco, Tunisia, Iraq, Iran, Lebanon, Saudi Arabia, Turkey, Algeria, and Egypt. Extremist Islam is intensely concerned with political power and eventually aims at world domination.

It has even shown up in the state of Israel, revealing itself in the influence of the New York *yeshivoth* and of the Lubavitch rabbis on Israeli politics. Religious political parties have wielded great influence in Israel, to the exasperation of the young atheistic sabras.

A similar concept permeates the various New Age movements that exalt humanity to a divine status. "You shall be like gods" (Gen. 3:5), Satan said. The old temptation that burned through the first pages of the Bible again lures modern masses. Like a tidal wave, it sweeps thousands of men and women to its bosom.

The king of the north gathers together all religious movements that in any way exercise political power under the cover of godly intentions, as well as all organizations promoting heaven on earth, while burying all hopes of a heavenly kingdom.

Recent political developments confirm Daniel's prophecy only too well. The world's leaders dare to merge their powers in a "New World Order," a development one could hardly have imagined a few years ago. It has all happened so fast! The indestructible iron curtain has fallen. Hard-core Communism is but a memory. The old utopia of Babel has revived, and unity is again a possibility. All we need is a leader, accepted by all, and to be fair, independent of nations judged too powerful.

The battle described by the prophet does not directly concern the modern state of Israel. The Temple no longer exists. Some picture Armageddon in a Palestine surrounded by bloodthirsty Arabs. At first glance it seems so biblical! A movie could even be made of it! But Armageddon has nothing to do with modern Israel. Armageddon is our battle. It is the struggle between two mentalities, two conceptions of happiness and religion. On the one hand, we have God, faith in His creation, and the conviction that humanity depends on Him for salvation and happiness. It is the hope in the kingdom of heaven. On the other hand is the illusion of our self-sufficiency, of our power to build a world of peace and happiness. The struggle is as old as the world. From the seductive branches of the tree in Eden it has spread down the succeeding ages to the present. It is the struggle of every person at the moment of decision to come back to God. The battle of Armageddon will wage at its worst in the last days when, in the midst of the crowds ablaze with their faith in gods of flesh and concrete, the people of God will grasp at the invisible God of hope. The real battlefield is the whole world.

STRUCTURE OF DANIEL 11

Introduction (verse 1)
> Flashback to the first year of Darius the Mede (cf. 9:1)

I. **The Persian-Greek Conflict (verses 1-4)**
1. Three Persian kings
2. Fourth king, rich against Greece (Artaxerxes)
3. A mighty king (Alexander); division into four kingdoms (Hellenistic period)

II. **The North-South Conflict (verses 5-39)**
> A   South attacks North (verses 5-8)
>> B   North attacks South (verses 9, 10)
>>> C   South attacks North (verses 11, 12)
> A$_1$ North attacks South (verses 13-25a)
>> B$_1$ South attacks North (verses 25b-27)
>>> C$_1$ North attacks South (verses 28-39)

III. **The "Time of the End" (verses 40-45)**
> A   South attacks North (verse 40a)
>> B   North attacks South (verses 40b, 41)
> A$_1$ North attacks North (verses 42, 43a)

B_1 South allies itself to the North against the "holy mountain"
Victory from above: end of the North

---

[1] Some commentators include the name of Smerdis the impostor (521), a suggestion of the Neoplatonist Porphyry, borrowed recently by E. J. Bickerman, *Four Strange Books of the Bible: Jonah, Daniel, Koheleth, Esther* (New York: 1967), pp. 117ff. We have chosen to omit him for several reasons: 1. He reigned less than a year (seven months); 2. He was an impostor originating from Media, and the prophecy speaks of Persian kings; 3. It is very probable that he never existed and was just a rumor concocted by Darius to justify his ascension to the throne. Herodotus would have accepted and recorded the official version. Isaac Asimov refers to it as perhaps "one of those cases where a great lie has been foisted on history" (*The Near East: 10,000 Years of History* [Boston: 1968], p. 125). In fact, numerous commentators overlook Smerdis (see L. F. Hartman and A. A. Di Lella, *The Book of Daniel, Anchor Bible*, [Garden City: 1978], p. 288).

[2] Such as Ibn Ezra, Ralbag, Ibn Yachiah, Malbim, etc. See also *Rosh Hashanah* 2b.

[3] Boniface and Marechal, *Histoire: Orient-Grèce*, p. 99; cf. pp. 198, 199. See also the testimony of Greek historians Thucydides (in *History of the Peloponnesian War*); Diodorus of Sicily 11. 71, 74, 77; Herodotus 6. 106.

[4] Some versions use the word "descendants," a translation of the feminine word *aharith* (here "after," as "descendant"). This word *(aharith)* is, however, never used in the plural form in the Bible (see Ps. 37:38; 109:13; Prov. 20:21; Eccl. 7:8; Eze. 23:25).

[5] See Lacocque, *The Book of Daniel*, p. 61, and Delcor, *Le Livre de Daniel*, p. 220; cf. also Rashi and Ibn Ezra in *Miqraoth Gdoloth*.

[6] Our approach remains outside the traditional line of interpretation. From the anti-Christian Neoplatonist Porphyry (300 C.E., see appendix) until today, rationalist critics have read this passage as referring to the war between the Seleucids (king of the north) and the Ptolemies (king of the south) that raged on until the reign of Antiochus Epiphanes (verses 21-45). Conservative exegetes have retained this interpretation of the conflict between the Ptolemies and the Seleucids and of Antiochus Epiphanes but have applied it to different sections of the text. According to them, only verses 5-13 allude to the conflict between Ptolemies and Seleucids, while verses 14-30 would point to either Rome or Antiochus Epiphanes. Verses 31-39 have in mind the power described in Daniel 8 as the little horn, and verses 40-45 would then apply to either Turkey or the Papacy (F. D. Nichol, ed., *The Seventh-day Adventist Bible Commentary*, rev. ed. [Washington, D.C.: 1979], vol. 4, pp. 868, 869, 876, 877; cf. William H. Shea, *Selected Studies on Prophetic Interpretation*, Daniel and Revelation Committee Series [Lincoln, Neb: 1982], vol. 1, pp. 44-55). In any case, the problem remains unsolved. The great diversity of interpretations regarding this passage testifies to a general state of confusion, and to the inconclusive character of the solutions. As for the spiritual and eschatological interpretations defended in our commentary, they are confirmed by reliable sources such as C. F. Keil, *Biblical Commentary of the Book of Daniel*, Commentary on the Old Testament (Grand Rapids: reprint 1991), vol. 9, p. 421; E. B. Pusey, *Daniel the Prophet* (New York: 1885), p. 136; and are implicitly supported by Ellen G. White (see *Testimonies for the Church* [Mountain View, Calif.: Pacific Press Pub. Assn., 1948], vol. 9, pp. 14-16).

[7] See Jer. 3:19; Eze. 20:6, 15; cf. Zech. 7:14; Ps. 106:24.

[8] The immediate context of verse 28 suggests that the king of the north is the subject of the verb "to return" *(shuv)*. The preceding verse (27) mentions two kings, already implying that the king of the north was at the side of the king of the south. In the next verse (29) the verb "to return" *(shuv)*, which is related to the king of the north, echoes the verb "to return" *(shuv)* in verse 28. It is because the king of the north was returning home that

his attack on the king of the south is described as a "return."

[9] A figure of speech technically called a "merismus."

[10] See also Isa. 43:6, 7; 1 Chron. 26:17; Ps. 107:3; Eccl. 1:6; S. of Sol. 4:16, etc. The ancient Egyptian chronicles use the same language to refer to Artaxerxes as the "king of the south and of the north," that is, king of the whole world (Robert William Rogers, *A History of Ancient Persia: From Its Earliest Beginnings to the Death of Alexander the Great* [New York: 1929], p. 176).

[11] See also 2 Kings 18:21; Jer. 2:18; etc.

[12] See Lacocque, p. 166.

[13] Cf. Isa. 11:14 and Jer. 25:21, where the three countries appear in the same order as a way of suggesting movement from the south to the north in the same context of a military campaign.

[14] See Num. 34:6, 12.

[15] See Isa. 2:2; Ps. 68:17; 132:13; etc.

[16] See Matt. 9:35; Mark 1:14; Luke 4:43; 8:1; Acts 1:3; 8:12; Col. 4:11; etc.

THE VICTORY
OF JERUSALEM

The book of Daniel speaks of wars and massacres, victims and oppressors. Our questions about them, though, remain unanswered. Then the words of chapter 12 suddenly jolt us. The last chapter is the shortest (only 13 verses versus the average 25 verses encountered in the other chapters). Its brevity is all the more striking as a particularly long chapter (45 verses) precedes it. The book finishes as it had begun. The length of chapter 2 (49 verses) also emphasizes the brevity of chapter 1 (21 verses). In Hebrew literature the conclusion always echoes the introduction. The circle is fully drawn, and we are at the end of the story. The structure of chapter 12 parallels that of chapter 7, the geometrical center of the whole book. Chapter 12 echoes chapter 7, following an inverse sequence (chapter 12: C_1, B_1, A_1 / chapter 7: A, B, C), according to a chiastic structure characteristic of Daniel's style.

C_1 (Daniel 12:1a), which describes the coming of the great heavenly prince Michael, corresponds in chapter 7 to C (Dan. 7:13, 27), the coming of the Son of man on the clouds of heaven. The stylistic expression "at that time" (Dan. 12:1) introduces this first section.

B_1 (Dan. 12:1-3), where books are consulted and where judgment is made between the wise and the not-so-wise, corresponds in chapter 7 to B (Dan. 7:9, 10, 26), the scene of judgment and the opening of the books. "At that time" (Dan. 12:1b) also introduces this section.

A₁ (Dan. 12:4-12), which concerns the little horn, corresponds in chapter 7 to A (Dan. 7:8, 25), which also speaks of the little horn. Allusions to both chapters 7 and 8 refer to the little horn. The link to chapter 7 occurs in the mention of "a time, times and half a time" (Dan. 12:7; cf. 7:25). The allusion to chapter 8 appears (1) in the appearance of the same heavenly being who asks the same question: "How long?" (Dan. 12:6; cf. 8:13); (2) the same achievements of the little horn, *niphlaoth* in Daniel 8:24 (translated by "astounding devastation") and *pelaoth* in Daniel 12:6 (translated by "astonishing things"); and (3) the same abolition of the daily sacrifice (Dan. 12:11, 12; cf. 8:11, 13). The expression "but you, Daniel" (Dan. 12:4) introduces the third section.

In the conclusion of the chapter (verse 13), the expression "as for you" encompasses both Daniel ("but you") and the whole of humanity.

I. The Rising of Michael

Everything points to the end, including both form and content. The first vision is dense with events, the violence of which we already see hinted at by the first verb, "will arise" *(amad)*. The Hebrew word belongs to the vocabulary of warfare and is performed by the soldier who resists and overcomes his enemy.[1] Here it responds to the multiple *amads* initiated by the kings of chapter 11 (verses 2-4, 6-8, 11, 13-17, 20, 21, 25, 31). The last occurrence of *amad,* the *amad* of final victory, is initiated by Michael, whose name is already a sign of victory: "who is like God!" The victory of Nebuchadnezzar in chapter 1 has its answer in the ultimate victory of Michael, Prince of Jerusalem. And with His victory, that of His people is ensured, a lesson given through a play on words that form the *inclusio* of chapter 12. The "rising" *(amad)* of Michael in the beginning of the chapter (Dan. 12:1) has its echo in the "rising" *(amad)* of the resurrected at the end of the chapter (verse 13). The victory is cosmic. It is not only a political or a religious triumph, but it is life defeating death.

The victory is all the more glorious because it has for its background a period of intense suffering and despair, "a time of distress such as has not happened from the beginning of nations" (verse 1).

We have no knowledge as yet of the nature of the despair that will torment the last survivors of human history. It has no historical precedent. And yet, the expression itself is not unique. "Distress" (or "trouble") occurs many times in the Old Testament (cf. Isa. 33:2; Jer. 14:8; 15:11; 30:7; Ps. 37:39), especially in the book of Jeremiah, where the same Hebrew expression "time of distress" appears three times and Jeremiah 30 describes it as an event out of the ordinary: "How awful that day will be! None will be like it. It will be a time of trouble for Jacob" (Jer. 30:7).

The context of Jeremiah 30 is a prediction of Israel's exile and consequently the despair and anguish of the exiled people. In the New Testament Jesus makes the same prediction through an explicit reference to the "prophet Daniel": "For then there will be a great distress, unequaled from the beginning of the world until now—and never to be equaled again" (Matt. 24:15, 21).

The time of the end would then be like that of the exile, a period when Jerusalem and the Temple are no longer in existence to guarantee salvation, a time when God is absent. Already the prophet Ezekiel had described the exile in such terms in a vision of the departure of the throne of God (Eze. 10). God's people find themselves crushed in the iron grip of Babylon. It is the experience of the absurd, where faith remains without an object. We are alone. God seems to have disappeared. History becomes a battlefield of raging forces, and evil seems to have triumphed over good. Why go on? Doubts smother the feeble flame of faith. With nowhere to turn, God's people seem to have no hope left. It is truly "a time of distress."

Never have we come so close to the events portrayed by the prophecy. And never have we been so indifferent. A brief summary of what we know only too well will suffice. The ecologists[2] watch the disintegration of our planet, but no one seems willing to do anything about it. Economists can hardly overcome their pessimism. World unemployment is on the rise. Three fourths of the population of the world face the real danger of death from hunger. Of course, we are only too accustomed to such numbers—they hardly bother us anymore. The little children with protruding ribs and stomachs disappear with a click of the remote control—until the day they will reappear in our own kitchens.

The political situation rests on shaky ground. Peace is indeed a goal as world powers meet with each other. But the weapons remain, buried underneath a mass of treaties and organizations. We live in the shadow of the atomic cloud. No country is not somehow involved in one conflict or another. All political action has repercussions on the international scene.

As for the moral state of our society, it is hardly recognizable, so disfigured it has become by crime, rape, drugs, alcohol, and AIDS. It spares no one as it affects all levels of society. Simultaneously, a new race of men and women has appeared: the professionals of success. Whatever artistic and moral ideals we once had have been replaced by the one ideal of our society, the only one worth striving for: money. Virtue is now proportional to performance. Modern humanity wills itself to become more and more efficient and less and less human.

Our civilization brews the worst disasters. And yet we are alive and well. We still walk the streets of our cities. Television still croons the reassuring words and images of our prosperity; and if not, it is just a movie anyway! We recycle. We exercise. We close our eyes and meditate, unwilling to face the slow putrefaction of our decadent society and preferring to ignore the slogans of a few eccentrics. After all, our leaders all speak in reassuring tones, and the people nod in their sleep.

And the flowers of evil sprout everywhere. The vision of Daniel is cosmic and concerns the "nations" (Dan. 12:1). No land, no island, no remote tribe can escape. It is a true "time of distress."

II. The Judgment

But the curtain does not fall on tragedy. The book of Daniel sees a "time of distress" through the perspective of divine hope.

Beyond the time of distress experienced by the exiles, the prophet Jeremiah foresees the return and the salvation of Israel: "It will be a time of trouble for Jacob, but he will be saved out of it" (Jer. 30:7).

Jesus predicts the coming of the Son of man: "Immediately after the distress of those days. . . . At that time the sign of the Son of man will appear in the sky" (Matt. 24:29, 30).

Likewise in Daniel 12, salvation from above interrupts the distress: "But at that time your people—everyone whose name is found written in the book—will be delivered" (verse 1).

As in chapter 7, chapter 12 places the coming of Michael (the Son of man) in a context of judgment. There also, the books are opened (Dan. 12:1; cf. 7:10). But in chapter 12 the judgment expands beyond the heavenly scene of chapter 7. We now witness its effect on earth as God takes concrete measures to deal with evil. We now realize that everything that ever happened *was* meaningful, that every event had implications. Everything was recorded and is being evaluated now. Judgment separates the wise from the wicked, life from death. Only radical change can clear the way for a new life. And only the eradication of death will make this new life possible. The judgment is cosmic and definite. Salvation will touch everything and will occur at a definite moment in history. "Multitudes who sleep in the dust of the earth will awake: . . . Those who are wise will shine like the brightness of the heavens, . . . like the stars for ever and ever" (Dan. 12:2, 3).

It takes courage to accept this. Salvation implies death. To be resurrected, we must first die. But the reward is real, palpable, and not some ethereal sort of immortality.

Biblical hope goes beyond human hope. It is not content to make vague promises of a better world, founded on human willpower. Rather, it points to a world in which the stars will shine eternally. Indeed, the reality of immortality will be more glorious than we can dare imagine: "No eye has seen, no ear has heard, no mind has conceived what God has prepared for those who love him" (1 Cor. 2:9).

III. How Long?

But for now, from the depths of our darkness, we may only yearn: "How long?" The question is stated twice in the book, once by Daniel, once by the angel. Daniel 12 answers it by presenting three periods of time. The first is already familiar to us: "a time, times and half a time" (verse 7). It is the period mentioned in chapter 7 during which the little horn would exert its oppressing power and lasting until 1798. Yet Daniel remains perplexed. "I did not understand" (Dan. 12:8). He wants to know more about the time of the end: "What will the outcome of all this be?"

The next two periods cover approximately the same length of time (1290 days and 1335 days) and are related to the first period (1260 days). Like the 1260 days, the 1290 and 1335 days should be understood in terms of years.

Furthermore, the way the 1290 days and the 1335 days are related places them in the same perspective, the second prolonging the first. "From the time that the daily sacrifice is abolished and the abomination that causes desolation is set up, there will be 1,290 days. Blessed is the one who waits for and reaches the end of the 1,335 days" (Dan. 12:11, 12).

If the 1290 days and the 1335 days have the same starting point (when the daily sacrifice is abolished), the first period would end after 1290 days, while the other would continue until the completion of 1335 days. The final destination is then 1335 days. The last period mentioned, it occurs in answer to the question "How long?" (verse 6; cf. verse 8). We remember this question from chapter 8. The same Hebrew words, *ad matay,* appear in the same context of "astonishing things" (*pelaoth,* 8:13, 24), and of dialogue between the two heavenly beings (verse 13; cf. 12:6). Finally, the being who states the question is none other than the high priest officiating at Kippur, one of the key themes of chapter 8. Indeed, the two visions speak of the same event. The 1335 days and the 2300 evenings and mornings answer the same question, "How long?" and consequently lead to the same time of the end, that is, 1844.

In the vision of 2300 evenings and mornings, Daniel understands the period of time beginning in 1844 as a heavenly Kippur, during which God judges the human race and prepares the kingdom to come. Then in the vision of 1335 days Daniel sees the same period of time, only he is now looking to the earth, to the person on it who "reaches the end" and whose happiness lies in waiting: "Blessed is the one who waits" (Dan. 12:12). The period of time beginning in 1844 is not only a time of fulfillment but of waiting and of hope.

Likewise, the Israelite would wait and hope during the festival of Kippur, as stated by the famous *De profundis:*[3] "I wait for the Lord, my soul waits, and in his word I put my hope. My soul waits for the Lord more than watchmen wait for the morning. . . . O Israel, put your hope in the Lord" (Ps. 130:5-7).

It is now possible, from the given number of 1335, to finally solve the enigma that had so disturbed the prophet, and to double-check the date of 1844. All the pieces of the puzzle are now at our disposition. Let us now review our conclusions. With 1844 being the endpoint of the 1335 days, we can calculate the starting point of the 1335 days simply by subtracting 1335 from 1843 (and not from 1844, which would include the year in course). The answer is 508 C.E., which confirms our date of 1798 as the endpoint of the 1290 days (508 plus 1290 equals 1798). According to our passage, 508 is then the time of the abolition of the daily sacrifice, clearing the way for the "abomination that causes desolation" (Dan. 12:11). The two events are not the same. The first paves the way for the second. Literally, the text says that the daily sacrifice is abolished "with the purpose" of establishing in its place the "abomination that causes desolation" (verse 11; cf. 11:31). In the book of Daniel the technical expression "abomination that causes desolation" designates the oppressing power (Dan. 8:11, 13; 9:27; cf. Matt. 24:15; Mark 13:14). According to the prophet, oppression would then last "a time, times and half a time," that is, 1260 day-years. The period covered by the 1260 years ends in 1798. Its starting point is then the year 538 (1798 minus 1260 equals 538). We have already encountered the dates 508, 538, and 1798 in chapter 7 of our commentary.

In 508 the medieval church reinforced its political status with the help of Clovis, king of the Franks (481-511) and eliminated the Arian tribes that had threatened its survival. From now on, "the Papacy may proceed unhindered to secure its political influence."[4]

But not until 538 does the emperor Justinian (527-565) definitely remove the Arian threat. As prophesied by Daniel, the appearance of the little horn depended on the fall of several kingdoms left over from the Roman Empire.

In 1798 the arrest and deportation of the pope himself finally curtails the political power of the medieval church.

The date of 1844 is a little harder to elucidate. Historically, not a lot happened on it. No revolution, no conquest, no decree occurred. It does not even figure in history manuals. Yet it seems to have some significance for Daniel. The year 1844 is one characterized by a movement both multiconfessional and international that situates itself precisely in a perspective of hope and waiting for the coming, the "advent" of God.[5]

Historian John B. McMaster estimates that nearly 1 million people out of the 17 million in the United States were involved in the movement.[6] Amazingly, Jews and Muslims had caught the same religious fever. On the Jewish side in the Hasidic movements of eastern Europe many expected the *Mashiah* to come in 5603 (1843/1844).[7] The Baha'i Muslims reached the same conclusion. The *bab* ("the door," opening to the hidden *iman*) had appeared in the year 1260 of the *hegira,* that is, in 1843/1844.[8] At the same time, in the secular world Marxist movements had begun to blossom, calling for progress and singing hope in another melody. Whatever reasons may explain this historical phenomenon, it is interesting that it happened in tune with the prophecy. It was a symptom of intense longing and waiting.

IV. The Way of the Wait

This "intense waiting" is already far behind us, and it has lost its freshness. We do not wait anymore, nor do we know how to wait. And yet today as the goal draws closer, we have still more reasons to wait and more need to hope. Waiting is the only way to survive. It is the last message Daniel hears from the angel: "Blessed is the one who waits" (Dan. 12:12).

Daniel's happiness is rooted in his waiting. But what he waits for remains on the horizon. His eyes will not see the Promised Land. Like Moses on Mount Nebo (Deut. 34:1), he remains behind. He can but grasp at the fleeting vision.

And yet he knows that the end is certain. The prophet will spend his lifetime waiting for an event that lies centuries away. Waiting is the essence of his existence. Exiled, he waits for the return. Inspired, he waits for the fulfillment of his vision. To wait is also the goal of the prophecy—it predicts even the wait itself.

But the waiting is not to be passive. The angel concludes: "As for you, go your way till the end" (Dan. 12:13). The book of Daniel concludes on the tragic note of the end. But this waiting does not consist of indifference. It is, on the contrary, a walk forward, a way of action and of life.

It is the waiting that makes the walking possible. Significantly, the prophecy relates the "rising" of the resurrected to Daniel's walking. "Go your way till the end" (verse 13). "Walk," "move on," recommends the angel, and "then at the end of the days you will rise to receive your allotted inheritance" (verse 13). Daniel can walk because he waits—because he is able to "see" the final destination, the resurrection "at the end of the days."

These last words of the angel carry the whole weight of the book of Daniel, and the message to Daniel is also for everyone. The personal end of Daniel (verse 13a) merges in the cosmic "end of the days" (verse 13b). The same Hebrew word *qetz* (end) appears in both instances. Also the last words of the angel transcend the person of Daniel and become universal. The particular "you, Daniel" (verses 4, 9) becomes the universal "you" (verse 13). Through Daniel God addresses the whole of humanity. For everyone is, like Daniel, bound to come to his or her end and die. Everyone is, like Daniel, locked in the hopeless civilization of Babel. Whether one waits or not, men and women, rich and poor, Jew, Christian, and Muslim—everyone is dreaming of something else. Everyone is, like Daniel, a Jewish prince in exile.

STRUCTURE OF DANIEL 12

I. The coming of Michael (verse 1a)

"At that time" (verse 1a)

- ◆ great chief
- ◆ time of distress

II. Judgment (verses 1b–3)

"At that time" (verse 1b)

- ◆ books open
- ◆ resurrection

III. Until When? (verses 4–12)

"And you Daniel" (verse 4)

- ◆ a time, times and half a time
- ◆ 1290 days
- ◆ 1335 days

IV. From the waiting to the walking (verse 13)

"And you" (verse 13a)

- ◆ end of Daniel
- ◆ end of days

---

[1] See Joshua 21:44; 23:9; Judges 2:14; 1 Sam. 6:19, 20; 17:51; 2 Sam. 1:10; 2 Kings 10:4; Jer. 40:10; etc.

[2] See the address by Gordon R. Taylor, *Le Jugement Dernier* (Calmann Levy, 1970).

[3] A psalm is recited during the liturgy of Kippur (see "Prayers of Rosh Hashanah" in the *Shulkhan Arukh,* chap. CIC, p. 582). It seems to have drawn its inspiration from the festival itself, as is indicated by the technical phrase "all their sins" (cf. Lev. 16:21, 22).

[4] Walter Ullmann, *A Short History of the Papacy in the Middle Ages* (London: 1972), p. 37. "Towards the year 500, an institution of incontestable authority emerges. . . . The pope, great pontificate *(summus pontifex),* great priest *(summus sacerdos),* sometimes called . . . 'vicar of Christ' . . . is considered to have a reputation of exceptional prestige" (author's translation from Marcel Pacaut, *La Papauté des origines au concile de Trente* [Paris: 1976], p. 44).

[5] See Henri Desroche, *The Sociology of Hope,* trans. Carol Martin-Sperry (London: 1979), p. 61.

[6] J. B. McMaster, *A History of the People of the U.S. From the Revolution to the Civil War* (New York: 1920), vol. 7, p. 136.

[7] *Machiah Maintenant* Jan. 30, 1993.

[8] See Joshua 21:44; 23:9; Judges 2:14; 1 Sam. 6:20; 17:51; 2 Sam. 1:10; 2 Kings 10:4; Jer. 40:10; etc. C. Cannuyer, *Les Bahais,* p. 11.